1982

CHILD ABUSE:

Prevention and Treatment
Through Social Group Work

CHILD ABUSE:

Prevention and Treatment

Through Social Group Work

Julianne L. Wayne and Nancy C. Avery

With a Foreword

by Ralph L. Kolodny

Charles River Books, Inc.

Boston

1980

Published by Charles River Books, Inc.

One Thompson Square, Charlestown, MA 02129

Printed in the United States of America

Library of Congress Cataloging in Publication Data
Wayne, Julianne L.   Child abuse.

1. Child abuse–United States. 2. Social case work 3. Child
Abuse–Treatment–United States. 4. Child abuse–United
States–Prevention. I. Avery, Nancy C., joint author. II. Title.
HV741.W28 362.7'₁ 79-16169
ISBN O-89182-012-4
ISBN O-89182-013-2 pbk.

To all parents, with hope.
To our parents, with gratitude:

Carolyn and Richard Hoag

in loving memory of
Evelyn and Nathan Liebowitz

Acknowledgments

The major contributors were the group members themselves, who shared their sorrows and triumphs with each other and with us and who helped us better undertand the "why" of child abuse and neglect.

We thank Nancy B. Ebeling of the Boston Office of the Children's Protective Services of Massachusetts' Society for the Prevention of Cruelty to Children. It was under her administration as District Executive and with her encouragement and support that the agency staff members were able to learn about, practice and contribute knowledge to social group-work practice with nonnurturing parents. She co-authored "Differential Groupwork in a Protective Agency," originally published in *Child Welfare*, September/October 1976, the article from which Chapter 4 was developed. We acknowledge the participation in the writing of that article of the following social workers, all of whom were staff members of the Boston Office of the Children's Protective Services at that time: Ann L. Arvanian, Linda Husar, Dorian Moffitt and Virginia O'Connell. We also thank Margaret Myer for her notes as leader of the first remedial group and Shirl E. Fay, Mary Connally and Jane Heald Levine for their thoughtful contributions.

The outreach program described in Chapter 6 would not have existed without the leadership of Phyllis Cosand. As a result of her tenure as Executive Director of the Crittenton Hastings House of the Florence Crittenton Division of the Child Welfare League, this and other important services were developed for pregnant women and mothers.

We are indebted to Leslie Zheutlin, our editor, for her faith in the value of what we had to say and for her talent in helping us say it. We appreciate the input of Ralph Kolodny, master group worker, who never said no to our requests for a share of his critical thinking. We thank Mary V. Murphy, our secretary, for her skill in translating pages that looked like road maps with crooked arrows into a legible manuscript.

Several chapters of this book are revisions of articles that appeared separately in various journals. We thank the editors for permission to reprint. They are as follows:

Chapter 4: Julianne L. Wayne, Nancy B. Ebeling, Nancy C. Avery, "Differential Groupwork in a Protective Agency," *Child Welfare,* Vol. LV, #8, Sept./Oct. 1976, pp. 581 - 591.

Chapter 5: Nancy C. Avery and Julianne L. Wayne, "Group Development and Grief Therapy for Non-Nurturing Mothers," *Social Work With Groups,* Vol. 1, #3, Fall 1978, pp. 287-298.

Chapter 6: Julianne L. Wayne, "A Group Work Model to Reach Isloated Mothers: Preventing Child Abuse," *Social Work With Groups,* Vol. 2, #1, Spring 1979, pp. 7-18.

Chapter 8: Julianne L. Wayne and Nancy C. Avery, "Activities as a Tool for Group Termination," *Social Work,* Vol. 24, #1, Jan. 1979, pp. 58-62.

Finally, we are grateful for the support of our husbands, Murray Wayne and Jim Avery, and for the delightfulness of Raymie Wayne, who patiently shared mommy with "the book". We welcome to the world James T. Avery, IV, who waited until the final stages of writing to be born.

Julianne L. Wayne
Nancy C. Avery

Note

Unless specifically referring to a female, the pronouns in this book have been written in the traditional masculine form. The English language has yet to develop a generic pronoun that equally recognizes women and men. We feared that use of a popular alternative such as "he/she" would be cumbersome to read and we chose to eliminate anything that might divert from the message of the book. This message is addressed with equal fervor to the betterment of men and women.

Contents

FOREWORD

The word "pleasure" may seem a strange one to use in connection with a book on social work with women who are unable to mother their children without neglecting or physically hurting them. Yet this book has to be a pleasure to read for any social worker who has practiced and taught professionally. The pleasure stems from three sources. First, it is clear from the manner in which Wayne and Avery write that they empathized with these mothers and were able to identify with them. Mental-health specialists from social work and its sister disciplines, psychiatry and psychology, have for the past twenty years and more called for therapists to understand abusing parents as "hurt children", acting out their own sense of deprivation and loss. One finds no monsters being admonished in this book, even under the guise of therapeutic guidance. Clearly, these practitioner-authors, as alert as they are to psychopathology and as free as they were of any illusions about their group members' capacity to act toward their children in physically and emotionally hurtful ways, were able to muster warm feelings toward them.

Another source of pleasure for the professional reader is the clarity of the writing and the honesty of the presentation. The authors say what they mean, and the reader is readily able to form images of situations and behaviors they describe. Abstractions are aplenty. Wayne and Avery are never pedestrian in their thinking, but they make sure, at every possible juncture, to buttress or explain a general idea with a specific case example. In their desire to inform and teach the reader, rather than simply to impress him, they also expose the less effective aspects of their efforts. When a group finally shakes down to a regular membership of only a few, the authors make it clear to the reader that the group worked with is small. We are left with no uncertainty as to its size. The numbers dealt with in each group were modest. This detracts in no way from the importance of the work done with them. That the authors realize this and feel in no way compelled to hide the actual numbers involved in each group is not only refreshing but gives aid and comfort to fellow practitioners who are helped thereby to have realistic expectations around matters of size, attendance and the like.

Finally, the pleasure in reading the book resides in the fact that what one obtains from it is a substantial picture of the social worker at his or her best, as a thinker-doer, a promoter of humane relationships among people, neither naive nor cynical, steeped in the literature of the field, and guided in her encounters with those she is to help by what she has drawn from the systematic thinking of others.

Group workers can look forward to finding in this book an approach which is anchored to a particular view of the stages through which groups and their members pass in the course of their development. The drama and tragedy of abusive mothers calls for neither pathos nor uncontrolled anger. They demand that the social worker in the group rely on a conceptual map regarding how individuals use each other in groups so that her responses may be helpful. The authors make their conceptual map clear and in so doing make it useful to the reader. Caseworkers will be reminded, through association, of the similarities between much of what they see in the way of the working through of grief by individual clients and what occurs as a result of interaction among members in a group of abusive mothers when guided by a sensitive social worker. Administrators will find ideas in abundance regarding the development of a groupwork program for women such as these and their families. Wayne and Avery are generous with their ideas, and these carry considerable weight precisely because they have implemented and tested them.

All social workers who are interested in groups and the potential of group work and group therapy for the treatment of those emotionally disturbed individuals whose behavior actively causes trouble for others will discover in this book a host of notions regarding the ameliorative and curative forces at work in groups. The key word is "creativity". Wayne and Avery are keenly aware of the need for differential use of groups. This includes not only the creation of different types of groups for those who have varying capacities to share feeling or to tolerate the absence of significant figures but also the use of the same group in a different stage of its development. Their description of how they employed crafts activities during the termination phase of a remedial group whose members had for months devoted themselves intensely to discussion of interpersonal problems, including hurting their children, is but one example. It is with such examples that these authors challenge us to design programs for those who abuse which will convey our confidence that they have some capacity for both self-control and satisfaction as parents. Read-ers will find that this book excites both their interest in the challenge and their desire to meet it.

Ralph L. Kolodny
Professor, Boston
University School of
Social Work
August, 1979

Chapter 1
Historical Overview

Child abuse and neglect are a part of human history. Through the eighteenth century, children were killed, abandoned, beaten, terrorized and sexually misused for a variety of socially sanctioned reasons. It was commonly believed that abusive treatment was necessary for discipline, for education, to please the gods and to drive away evil spirits. Infanticide was a means to gain population control or to rid families of unwanted offspring. Mutilation and sexual molestation were occasionally practiced as initiation into manhood or womanhood. Disfigurement or amputation were often used to heighten children's effectiveness as beggars. The social acceptance of violence toward children lead Lloyd De Mause, in *The Nightmare of Childhood*, to conclude that "a very large percentage of children born prior to the eighteenth century were what would today be termed battered children."[1]

As battered children grew up to batter, in turn, their own children, the general attitude of "spare the rod and spoil the child" became part of our socio-cultural heritage. In the seventeenth and eighteenth centuries beating instruments included whips of all kinds, shovels, canes, iron and wooden rods, bundles of sticks, the discipline (a whip made with small chains) and special school instruments like the flapper, which had a pear-shaped end and a round hole to raise blisters. Abusive treatment began early in infancy and occurred in all social classes. One mother wrote of a battle with her four-month-old: "I whipped him til he was actually black and blue, and until I could not whip him anymore, and he never gave up one single inch."[2] Beethoven whipped his pupils with a knitting needle and sometimes bit them.

The inferior status of European children influenced attitudes in Colonial America. England sent the homeless and poor children of London as indentured servants to provide cheap labor for settlement in the New World. The work the child could produce was valued much more highly than were his basic human rights. Colonial children were chattel and totally subject to their parents' will. In 1646 the Colony of Massachusetts passed the Mosaic Law providing the death penalty for unruly children:

If a man have a stubborn or rebellious son of sufficient years of understanding, viz sixteen, which will not obey the voice of his father or the voice of his mother, and that when they have chastened him will not harken unto them, then shall his father and mother, being his natural parents, lay hold on him and bring him to the magistrates assembled in Court, and testify to them by sufficient evidence that this their son is stubborn and rebellious and will not obey their voice and chastisement, but lives in sundry notorious crimes. Such a son shall be put to death.[3]

Even in the late 1800's, life for many American children, especially the poor, was brutal. They were beggars and street performers. Unwanted infants were sent to "baby farms", often to be put to death or to die from lack of care. Children were put to work in mills, mines and factories, where they suffered excessive abuses. Little, if any, attention was paid to their educational or physical well-being. Apprenticeship systems for boys approximated slavery. Many children lacked a familial environment and a nurturing parental relationship.

In the United States, public concern for the welfare of children began with the Mary Ellen case in the 1870's, when a church worker intervened to rescue a young girl who had been treated with shocking brutality by her foster parents in a New York City tenement. Because there were no laws protecting children from maltreatment, church leaders turned to the already existing Society for the Prevention of Cruelty to Animals. The SPCA was victorious in court, arguing that Mary Ellen, as a member of the animal kingdom, was entitled to the same protection from cruelty as an animal.

Mary Ellen's day in court was described by a famed newspaper writer and social reformer of the time, Jacob Riis:

I was in a court room full of men with pale, stern looks. I saw a child brought in, carried in a horse blanket, at the sight of which men wept aloud. I saw it laid at the feet of the judge, who turned his face away, and in the stillness of that court room I heard a voice raised claiming for that child the protection men had denied it, in the name of the homeless cur on the street.[4]

Mary Ellen, at 8 years of age, told the court:

> She [Mama] used to whip me with a twisted whip – a raw hide. The whip always left a black and blue mark on my body. I have now the black and blue marks on my head which were made by mamma, and also a cut on the left side of my forehead which was made by a pair of scissors. She struck me with the scissors and cut me; I have no recollection of ever having been kissed by anyone...

> Whenever mamma went out I was locked up in the bedroom...I have no recollection of ever being on the street in my life.

New York Times
April 10, 1874
The Case of Little Mary Ellen[5]

The court sentenced Mary Ellen's foster mother to prison for one year to do hard labor. Mary Ellen was sent to a shelter for homeless children.

The conscience of American society was aroused by the brutal treatment of Mary Ellen and laws were passed to protect children from maltreatment. The first society to protect children from neglect, abuse and exploitation was established in New York City in 1875 to enforce the laws against cruelty to children. In 1878 the Massachusetts Society for the Prevention of Cruelty to Children was chartered "for the purpose of awakening interest in the abuses to which children are exposed by the intemperence, cruelty, or stupidity of parents and guardians, and to help the enforcement of existing laws on the subject, and procure needed legislation for kindred work...[6] The protection of children from neglect and abuse began, not as a social service, but as a law-enforcement function. The focus was on removing children from neglectful and abusive parents and on punishing the parents for this treatment of their children.

> We have agents about the city to look after poor children in the streets. In cases where we find children are hired to beg, we arrest the parties who hire them out. This is frequently

done by Italian organ-grinders, of whom we arrested quite a number during the past month. The society in all its transactions in reference to children brings them before the court having jurisdiction in the matter. If a complaint is made to us of any child being ill used, we send an officer to investigate the case and see what can be done. If the child is very badly abused, we cause it to be taken away and put into an asylum or otherwise properly provided for.

William P. Letchworth,
Extract from Ninth Annual Report of the State Board of Charities of State of New York Relating to Orphan Asylums and other Institutions for Albany, 1876.[7]

In the early 1900's legislation and social programs reflected an expanding concern for the welfare of children. The first national legislation regulating and restricting child labor was passed by Congress (Owen-Keating Bill, 1916). In 1909 the first White House Conference on Children affirmed the value of one's own family. The Conference proclaimed that no child should be removed from his home for reasons of poverty alone, and it recognized that working with parents to prevent recurring neglect and abuse of children was a much-needed function of the child-protective agencies. The societies created to enforce laws for the prevention of cruelty to children began to provide services to help families better care for their children.

The History of Social-Work Intervention

The change in the focus of protective services was heavily influenced by two factors: the gradual shift in socio-cultural attitudes toward the more humane treatment of children, and the increased knowledge of human behavior and psychoanalytic concepts in the profession of social work.

The first social workers in the late nineteenth century were volunteer "friendly visitors" or paid "agents" whose purposes were to certify a family's need for financial aid and to promote the independence of the "worthy poor". Attitudes underwent subtle but important changes, from tacit blame of the poor for being shiftless or thriftless to recognition that men are born socially, intellectually and physically unequal. The idea of "the poor" gave way to the idea of "the client", defined by Mary Richmond as a person whose "character, physical condition or circumstances, or a combination of these, have made him incapable of full self-maintenance in his social setting."[8] The new methods and skills in social-work practice emphasized helping individuals assume more adequate social functioning.

A milestone in the development of professional casework was the publication in 1917 of Mary Richmond's *Social Diagnosis*. This book, the first organized presentation of its kind, set forth a systematic approach to the study and diagnosis of the client's problems and articulated what have become the basic tenets in casework, among them the need to individualize each client, the client's right to self-determination and the reciprocity of the client-worker relationship.[9]

Beginning in the 1920's and continuing for many decades, caseworkers immersed themselves in the study of Freud in an effort to understand human behavior. They sought to model their practice after that of dynamic psychiatry, which focused on the intrapsychic forces that shape behavior. The practice of social casework was concentrated on an individual's inner motivations rather than on his social interactions. Abusive and neglectful parents, however, did not fit the mold of the client who could readily respond to this approach. They rarely reached out for help with a presenting problem and as a rule were not intrapsychically oriented. As a result, caseworkers believed that these parents were totally different from others with problems in child care and rearing. They were viewed as unreachable through professional help.[10]

It was not until after the Depression of the 1930's and World War II that caseworkers began to re-examine the interrelationship between situational stress and an individual's ability to cope with problems. In psychiatry, many shifted their focus from the mysteries of the unconscious to those of the conscious mind. Casework practice entered a period of renewed interest in the connections between social circumstances and individual psychology.[11]

The Children's Division of the American Humane Association, which acts as a national association for both public and private child protective agencies, played a major role in having child abuse and neglect perceived as a result of social as well as psychological and moral influences.

> Today we do not necessarily cite parental failure to provide adequate care as wilful neglect. We recognize

neglect (or negligence) as a result, usually of the parent's immaturity, maladjustment or physical or mental illness and not infrequently as a result also of economic or social change over which the parent has no control. Protective service is a service to parents on behalf of their children and is directed not so much at rescuing the child from the home, as preserving, where possible, the home for the child.[12]

Protective workers incorporated into their practice the theories of personality dysfunction described and analyzed by Irving Kaufman, M.D., and Beatrice Simcox Reiner in their book, *Character Disorders in Parents of Delinquents*, published in 1959. The psychiatric classification of "character disorder" covers a wide range of disordered behaviors. Such individuals experience pervasive malaise and are driven to express their discomfort in impulsive behavior that is either self-destructive or socially inappropriate and unacceptable. They lack internal control and a sense of responsibility to others. They do not usually seek help of their own free will and are often resistant and distrustful of helping professionals.[13]

With the gradual merging of this theoretical base with social work values and practice, protective service programs became an integral part of social welfare. The maltreatment of children was not a widely recognized phenomenon, however, until the early 1960's, when the term "battered child" was popularized by C. Henry Kempe and his colleagues at the University of Colorado Medical Center. It was not until the 1960's that virtually every state passed legislation requiring or at least recommending reporting of suspected child abuse incidents. By the early 1970's elaborate but generally fragmented systems of child protection had developed in all the states. Despite variations in particular states and communities, the following elements are included: a mandatory reporting process, public and private child protective service, and various other agencies and individuals involved in identification, disposition or treatment of cases.[14]

Almost 100 years after the chartering of the first Society for the Prevention of Cruelty to Children, the Congress of the United States passed the Child Abuse Prevention and Treatment Act (1974). The act established a National Center on Child Abuse and Neglect and provided funds for research and treatment.[15]

Social workers continued to look for new ways to serve the parent population. As workers developed a growing appreciation of the importance of peer support and stimulation, and observed the devastating effects of isolation, they began to use group work as a treatment method. The trend toward group services began in the 60's, and in 1972 Robert Mulford wrote, "Protective services programs increasingly are organizing parent groups from the caseloads and offering opportunities for group discussion of subjects relating to child-rearing, marital relationships, homemaking, and so forth."[16]

The challenge for the social worker remains to help families accept social services in order to achieve a more satisfying level of functioning. In the process of helping parents constructively cope with the factors contributing to neglect and abuse, social workers find themselves applying the same knowledge, methods and skills they use in helping families cope with any of the psychosocial problems that adversely affect children and their parents.[17]

Neglect and Abuse Defined

Our socio-cultural attitudes toward child-rearing practices and society's response to the abusive treatment of children have changed dramatically in the past two centuries. In the process there have been differing opinions as to what constitutes neglect or abuse. One definition focuses on the outcome of acts; a second includes the element of the "intentionality" of the acts; and a third suggests that child abuse is a culturally determined label. The label is a function of the values, background and experiences of the labeler, as well as of the norms of the community in general.

Today, however, cultural differences and uneven community awareness of good child-rearing practices are giving way to a consensus on acceptable child care. The Child Abuse Prevention and Treatment Act defines child abuse and neglect as "the physical or mental injury, sexual abuse, negligent treatment, or maltreatment of a child under the age of 18 by a person who is responsible for the child's welfare under circumstances which indicate that the child's health or welfare is harmed or threatened thereby.[19]

Norman Polansky defines neglect as a "condition in which a caretaker responsible for the child either deliberately or by extraordinary inattentiveness permits the child to experience avoidable present suffering and/or fails to provide one or more of the ingredients generally deemed essential for developing a person's physical, intellectual and emotional capacities."[20] Physical abuse has been defined as any nonaccidental physical injury inflicted on a child by a parent (or other caretaker) deliberately or in anger. Emotional abuse and neglect are terms often used interchangeably to mean lack of love and proper direction, the inability to accept the child's limits and potential, the failure to encourage the child's normal development by assurances of love and acceptance, or the continued scapegoating and rejection of a specific child.

The social-work profession has both been influenced by and contributed to the progression toward more humane treatment of children and the growth of children's rights. This movement, however, may have inadvertently fostered the harsh treatment of abusive and neglectful parents who more often receive social and legal retribution than education or treatment. The maltreatment of children is surely a moral and legal problem, but it is also a symptom of the abuser's misery and suffering. In most instances these parents are themselves abused children grown older, and simply punishing them for their behavior is a form of blaming the victim. Sadder still is the reality that punitive actions work against the ultimate goal of protective services which is to help create and support a healthy family environment in which the child can be nurtured and helped to grow.

Issues of moral justice and mental health can become confused as professionals strive to meet the challenge described by Erikson as the wedding of moral indignation with clinical dispassion. To lose either is ultimately to lose both.

Chapter 2
Understanding the Causes of Child Abuse

Two major theoretical models have been developed as ways of understanding and thinking about child abuse. The first may be termed the "psychological" or "clinical" model. The focus of this approach is on identifying the personal factors that determine why one individual is abusive while another is not. The second of these two models may be termed a "sociological" model. Its primary emphasis is on identifying those socio-cultural conditions that affect the rate of child abuse within the United States as a whole or within particular subgroups.[1] These conceptual models are sometimes presented as if they are in conflict, although they are actually complementary. The historical process of defining child abuse as a problem has been influenced by the theoretical underpinnings of each of these models. We must continue to integrate these theories if we are to understand fully why people seriously and repeatedly neglect or abuse their children. The way an individual perceives a problem affects his response to it. Social workers must continue the historical trend toward conceptually integrating the internal and external influences on behavior, so that their interventions will reflect a broad holistic approach to the problem. Indeed, descriptive clinical studies of abusive families conclude that violent, destructive attacks on children result from many sources: (1) personality disorders of the parents, (2) personality disorders of the child, (3) family relationship problems, and (4) environmental stress.[2] In many instances the support of cultural norms can be added as a causative factor.

Traditional intervention has been based on the psychological model because the individuals referred for protective services are usually those with serious personality disorders, and clinically oriented protective workers respond at the behavioral level. Within this model are two streams of thought. The first is grounded in psychodynamically oriented personality theory. According to this "psychiatric" model, behavior is a function of personality traits or states of the individual, and deviant behavior, such as child abuse, is a symptom of an underlying "mental illness" or disease. The causes of the problem are found in the motivations behind the behavior. The second type of clinical model might be called a "social learning" or "behavioral" model. The emphasis in this approach is on the behav-

9

ior of the individual. Rather than viewing deviant behavior as symptomatic of underlying problems, this approach analyzes the behavior in terms of the environmental context in which it occurs.[3]

Studies indicate that abusive parents are the abused children of yesterday. Behavioral scientists have shown that individuals learn patterns of behavior and develop a sense of identity through early familial interactions. Dana Ackley states: "Our parents model parenting behavior for us more intimately than anyone else, and their patterns of raising us become so ingrained that we frequently repeat them without being aware of their source."[4] By our society's standards most abusive parents had poor parenting models and did not experience consistent positive parental interaction. Their parents did not see them as people with real worth and potential, and they incorporated the view of themselves as "black sheep" within their families. Children who experience hostile, violent attacks frequently identify with the aggressor, and when they become parents, they can justify abusive acts. "Psychologically he has a license from the superego to abuse his child, which is irrevocable, handed down to him at a time when he was abused by his original superego figure."[5] This is not to say that all abused children of today are the abusive parents of tomorrow. One's ability to cope with the demands and frustrations of parenthood and life's normal stresses is dependent on one's total life experiences.

The psychiatric view maintains, that because of the deficits in their original childhood experiences, abusive parents remain emotionally immature and expect their children to meet their own infantile needs. This sets in motion the pattern of parent-child role reversal. The concept of role reversal was introduced by Morris and Gould (1963), who defined it as "a reversal of the dependency role, in which parents turn to their infants and small children for nurturing and protection."[6] Unable to show tenderness, gentleness and empathy, the parents expect these behaviors from their children.[7] These unrealistic performance expectations are coupled with disregard for the infants' needs, limited abilities and helplessness. Many abusive parents use physical punishment to implement their high standards. Terrorized children become skilled at supplying their parents with comfort and physical caring. For example, the two-year-old who draws her chair to the ironing board in an attempt to help her mother, or the five-year-old who brings a tissue to her crying mother and comforts her, saying "It will be O.K., Mommy."

10

Most children, however, are incapable of filling their parents' overwhelming, unmet needs. As a result, these children remain the target of their parents' anger and frustration. Young children do not question the judgement of their parents, and they accept hostile criticism as affirmation of their own inadequacy.[8] They begin to view themselves as worthless and unworthy of positive attention, but they still maintain the hope of one day becoming lovable.

Children also generalize from their original familial experience. Because they have not learned to trust, they fear that all close relationships will produce disappointment and threats to their self-esteem. At the same time, they seek closeness to make up for the nurturance they never received. This push-pull pattern leads to the development of hostile-dependent relationships. The hunger for emotional support results in excessive dependency and unrealistic expectations of the significant others in their lives. Observable relationship patterns begin to emerge. Their feelings of inadequacy lead them to choose relationships with individuals who are as emotionally needy as themselves, and unable to provide the emotional support they seek. Disappointed, angry and indignant, they react with the criticism and rejection they are so used to receiving. A large number of abusing parents are simply recreating their dependent, yet angry, hating relationship with their own parents. The pattern continues to repeat itself because with each failure they are armed with further evidence of their inherent worthlessness.[9]

The repeated failure to establish a close relationship and the feelings of anxiety which closeness arouses in them result in emotional isolation. Norman Polansky documents that parents implicated in child neglect fit the sociological definition of alienation. He is not talking about alienation in its usual sociological context, that is, as a feature of lower-class status. He means, rather, alienation that has its roots in a sense of futility, in the despair and detachments of childhood which one's later life has done too little to ameliorate.[10] These parents feel, that they are different from others; that no one has experienced what they have. They do not reach out to potential sources of emotional support that might help them avoid hurting their children, because they feel that they are incapable of being helped.

Often an incident of abuse is precipitated by the presence of situational stress. Parents with a large residue of unfulfilled emotional needs are extremely sensitive to the withdrawal of any support in their environment and may completely lose control in the face of a

crisis. The seriousness of a crisis may range from an infant's cranki-
ness to a major tragedy. Whether or not a crisis precipitates abuse is
dependent on how close the parent is to losing control. The demands
of child rearing may become overwhelming to a mother when marital
conflict causes a father to slam the door and leave in anger. At that
moment the mother looks to her child for the understanding and
support she needs in her present situation. If the child then spills a
glass of milk or accidentally breaks a window, the mother's rage may
become out of control. Another mother may react to a similar crisis
by escaping into alcohol and emotionally deserting her child.

In contrast to the clinical, the sociological approach studies the
effects of socio-cultural variables on the rate of abuse in groups.
These variables include the effects of poverty, size of family, and cultural attitudes toward the use of violence and abuse.[11]

David Gil, in his book *Violence Against Children*, showed why individuals rarely adhere to one of these models without incorporating
concepts and variables associated with the other.

> ...the manner in which individual personality dis-
> orders are expressed and the content of neurotic and
> psychotic fantasies and symptoms in any given
> society, tend to be influenced by the sociocultural
> context in which they develop. Such disorders, fan-
> tasies, and symptoms tend to be extreme manifesta-
> tions of attitudes and behaviors which, at a less
> extreme level, constitute a normal element of the cul-
> ture and care sanctioned by it. In other words what
> society considers sick and deviant in human behvior
> is not necessarily qualitatively different from what it
> considers healthy and normal. The difference may be
> quantitative only. Thus it would seem that incidents
> of serious physical attack on children, which can be
> understood dynamically as symptoms of individual
> psychological disorders and/or environmental stress
> may at the same time be deeply rooted in culturally
> supported attitudes.[12]

Gil's research confirmed that our culture sanctions the discretional
right of parents and other caretakers of children to use physical force
in disciplining children. He cites the example of many state legisla-

tures giving teachers the discretional right to administer corporal punishment to children.[13]

If the two conceptual models are integrated, child abuse can be attributed to a wide range of factors. David Gil suggests a continuum running from incidents involving normal individuals, who are acting in a manner approved by their culture, while disciplining children in their care, to child abuse triggered by complicated personality disorders in various combinations with environmental factors.[14]

Social workers must understand the two conceptual models and their interrelationship in order to meet the differential needs of the nonnurturing population. The multidimensional nature of child abuse means that many disciplines and methods of service are required to meet the goal of improved parenting. To be effective, the total community must share responsibility for protective services. The agency with the primary responsibility must be able to offer supportive services, which include individual and family counseling, Parents Anonymous, day care or babysitting, family planning, homemaker services, health services, parent education, parent aids or lay therapists, short-and long-term foster care, job counseling, job training and referral, emergency financial assistance, adequate housing and the provision of transportation.

Group services have a special contribution to make to the lives of abusive parents, and this book will offer theory and examples from practice to support this assertion.

Chapter 3
The Special Value of Social Group Work

The literature on abusive and neglectful parents makes reference to their past and present isolation from peers and from the mainstream of their social environment. Yet the importance of interpersonal relations and of group membership are widely recognized by psychologists, who are in general agreement that healthy personality growth is characterized by the widening of the newborn's egocentric social circle as a result of his growing ability and need to interact with others. According to Irvin Yalom, "Group membership, acceptance and approval are of the utmost importance in the development of the individual. The importance of belonging to childhood peer groups, adolescent cliques, fraternities, the proper social "in" group can hardly be overestimated."[1]

It is through interpersonal transactions that the individual develops a sense of self, receives nurturance and is made to feel whole. Otherwise the emotionally starving individual may hurt others in the sometimes frantic quest for psychic survival. Whether the isolation and inability to develop satisfying relationships with others are causes or effects of the psychological dynamics expressed in non-nurturing parental behavior, they are surely factors that contribute to the destructive behavior of such parents toward their children. Gisela Konopka describes the importance of human relationships:

> An inseparable connection exists between self-respect and a freely given relationship with someone else. All his life, man struggles to gain or retain this sense of self by reaching to the *you* – to the one who gives importance and warmth and tenderness to his own self. When this bridge is built, he can give love to others and can accomplish whatever he is capable of doing. At that point he can feel fulfillment and achieve sacrifice. But without the bridge between the *I* and the *you*, the human being crumbles. He may either destroy himself or others in subtle or glaring forms.[2]

In his discussion of the human growth cycle, Erik Erickson considers the ability to parent an outgrowth of an earlier ability to relate to and care about others. He asserts that the adult must choose between generativity and stagnation:

> The fashionable insistence on dramatizing the dependence of children on adults often blinds us to the dependence of the older generation on the younger one. Mature man needs to be needed and maturity needs guidance as well as encouragement from what has been produced and must be taken care of.
>
> Generativity, then, is primarily the concern in establishing and guiding the next generation.[3]

In Erickson's developmental theory, the individual gains the ability to resolve each life stage's developmental tasks by building on the strengths and skills gained in previous life phases. The seeds of the social being are born within the infant and must be psychologically and socially nurtured in order to survive and grow. The social being that evolves will mature into an adult capable of investing in an intimate sexual relationship; from this relationship grows the ability to care about and for the offspring of that union.

Having a child does not in itself indicate the achievement of generativity. Erickson notes:

> In fact, some young parents suffer, it seems, from the retardation of the ability to develop this stage. The reasons are often to be found in early childhood impressions ... in the lack of some faith, some "belief in the species," which would make a child appear to be a welcome trust of the community.[4]

Professional intervention must focus on helping the nonnurturing parent to develop both a sense of trust and a sense of community. Through the professionally guided interpersonal transactions of social group work, alienated individuals can be helped to create and maintain a social system whose dynamics at certain stages resemble a family unit and at others, a microcosm of society at large. Each member is helped to successfully meet the interpersonal demands of the unfolding group experience and in so doing builds a long-overdue repetoire of life skills. Within the group context the individual can be nurtured, perhaps for the first time, can learn to contribute to the well-being of others, can incorporate new behavioral norms for parenting, and finally, can develop new parenting skills and abilities. In this way, the group experience serves as a laboratory or training ground for life itself.

As recognition of the mutuality of human needs and interests grows, and as group participation becomes more valued in our society, mental-health professionals increasingly use group approaches. Although more and more caseworkers in casework settings are starting to employ the group-work method, the rationale for this is usually only partially recognized in terms of the potential gains for clients. The common reasons offered include: (1) eagerness to save time and more quickly serve clients on a waiting list; (2) wanting to support a particular worker who is eager to work with a group; and (3) recognition of the benefits of peer support. Only the third of these reasons is based on the actual value of the group experience to its members.

The first reason is an efficiency factor that relates more to agency administration than to therapeutic benefits for clients. Yet in actuality the group meetings may be only a portion of the time required to practice group work successfully. It is difficult to begin and maintain most group experiences and this task is especially challenging when trying to serve a generally isolated population which has successfully avoided group involvement for most of their lives. The worker must be prepared to contact or meet with certain members individually between meetings if they are to be helped to stay in the group.

The second reason, worker interest, is based more on the worker's professional growth than on the client's mental health. Even so, this is not an unimportant factor. Enthusiasm and positive expectations of the professional directly relate to a client's progress.

The third reason, peer support, is a significant and legitimate client-centered reason to use groups; but that phrase, in and of itself, is too general to be of great help to the practitioner. In order to capitalize on the value of a group experience, the practitioner must identify the specific curative factors that make this approach different from one-to-one intervention. With awareness of these factors, the worker is better able to direct processes in order to maximize their benefits. This knowledge also contributes to a more appropriate process in selecting individuals for groups.

It is a vast oversimplification to speak about groups as if they all were alike. The literature of social group work is replete with comparisons of one kind of group to another. Group-therapy literature yields additional dimensions for consideration. In later chapters we will present various group-work models and describe their differential use in a protective agency. The differences in group approaches can be summarized by pointing out that groups can focus on interpersonal processes, on each individual's intrapsychic dynamics or on the achievement of a common group goal (as in the task-oriented group). Treatment can occur either within the group context or through group dynamics. Group workers may assume an active or passive stance and may use activities or dialogue as the primary means of expression and communication within the group. While these and other approaches have their benefits and deficits, all group experiences share aspects that are beneficial for this population. All group-work approaches are potentially therapeutic.

Curative Elements of a Group Experience

Through systematic questioning of group therapists and group-therapy patients, Irvin Yalom has identified and divided the curative factors of a group experience into ten primary categories. He says that they "operate in every type of therapy group. However, they assume a differential importance depending on the goals and compositions of the specific group; factors which are minor or implicit in one group approach may be major or explicit in another."[5]

As we review these factors and others, it becomes apparent that many of the categories overlap and are interdependent. Nevertheless, it serves a purpose to discuss Yalom's findings, to elaborate upon them and to relate them to the nonnurturing parent population.

1. *Imparting of Information*

Yalom refers to the imparting of information in its most direct sense – that is, the therapist offers didactic instruction, advice, suggestions, or direct guidance to help the client cope with life situations. He also indicates that therapists tend to devalue this aspect of group life. Yet work with abusive and neglectful parents reveals a surprising amount of ignorance and misinformation about child rearing and development, and a subsequent need for basic information. One abusive mother said she really didn't know that her four-month-old daughter did not understand the stress she created in the household by crying night after night. The mother said she needed to learn from the social worker and the other mothers that her infant's behavior was totally nonmalicious, that at four months she was incapable of learning not to cry from being hit.

The imparting of information can also occur through more subtle means than the direct transmission of information. It can occur through observations and reflections of life within the group. In any one meeting the group worker is called upon to react to a variety of personalities and situations and in so doing may convey messages of another sort. For example, at one group meeting a particular member was giving a boring monologue about her life situation and frustrated others who wanted to speak. The worker turned to this member and remarked, "Jean, it's hard for me to stay tuned in to your story when you don't stop and give me a chance to join you in the conversation." Jean was momentarily taken aback but soon perceived this as a positive remark and an indication of the social worker's interest in her. Shortly after that, another member said, "I should try that on my kid sometime – just telling him what I'm feeling instead of losing my temper." In this instance, the worker's behavior provided information about how to handle interpersonal stress. If the member had not recognized and articulated the quality of the transaction, the worker might have purposely pointed to that interaction or others within the group to illustrate alternative interpersonal behaviors. Teaching social skills through actual demonstration is also a form of imparting information.

2. *Installation of Hope*

Every group will contain members who are at varying phases of treatment. The members who are more advanced or "healthier" can serve as an inspiration to those who are more troubled. Even in the unlikely event that a group is composed of equally noncoping or regressed individuals, each one will have some area of functioning or instance of success that can be perceived as an achievement by the others. Every time a troubled parent hears "I used to do that too", she is confronted with someone's success. This becomes a source of inspiration that can only come from a peer. It is a strong component of all self-help groups, including Parents Anonymous.

3. *Universality*

Most abusive parents are filled with guilt and shame about their actions toward their children. Fortunately, they are correct in their belief and perception that most other parents do not behave as they do. They are mistaken, however, in their belief that *no* other parents act or feel as they do. Through the group experience, they quickly learn that they are not unique.

Arthur Blum writes about this phenomenon and refers to it as the "aha" response. "This response comes about as a result of recognition by the members that their private attitude, which may vary from the public norms of the group, is not unique and different. The surprise that is often expressed when group members suddenly discover that other people hold the same attitude they do and that these attitudes are not those commonly expressed in public, is what has been defined here as the aha' response."[6] Nonnurturing parents frequently express relief at learning that although one is supposed to be loving and caring to one's children, it is also possible to feel anger and even hatred. For many, this recognition of not being alone may be the first sense of being like others, of belonging to the human race.

4. *Altruism*

Webster defines this as "regard for and devotion to the interests of others: opposed to *egoism* and *selfishness*." The parents who enter into group services do not perceive themselves as contributing members of society – as people who are capable of selflessness. They are frequently filled with self-pity about the situation within which they find themselves. Their earliest recollections are of themselves as victims of forces beyond their control. With all their emotional energy directed inward, they have not been able to feel concern for others or to give of themselves to someone else. Many group members find themselves consoling or giving heartfelt advice to another human being for the first time. This experience modifies their self-concept from the unacceptable, unaccepted child to the caring, functioning adult. The ability to give and nurture can then be carried over into the parent-child relationship.

5. *The Corrective Recapitulation of the Primary Family Group*

We have already noted that in most instances abusive parents did not experience adequate parental nurturance. The group experience, however, offers an unusual opportunity to turn back time: to recreate the family situation and engage in a reparenting process.

James Garland, Hubert Jones and Ralph Kolodny reinforce the

notion of the group as family surrogate in their discussion of the third stage of group development, "intimacy": "As the character of group life becomes increasingly intimate, there are indications that the frame of reference for the experience becomes a familial one. References to siblings are more prevalent ... the worker may be referred to, often jokingly, as the 'Club Mamma' or 'Pop' ... where group members are permitted to bring a significant part of themselves into the group and to determine the character of the experience in relation to the safe, non-retaliatory framework initially set up by the worker, transference would seem to be one very natural outcome."[7]

The worker can use these familial transferences to promote growth. For many individuals it is this familylike environment that provides the support they need to recognize and give up their unreal hope and expectation that they will yet be miraculously loved and accepted by their original, natural family. This is an important point in the treatment of abusive parents and will be elaborated upon in Chapter 5.

JoAnn Cook and Sharrell Munce refer to the reparenting process by noting that within the group-treatment experiences they offered, abusive mothers were able to progress through individual psychosocial developmental phases. "Group members have been raised' in this new family which they have helped to create and with which they identify. Relationships in the group progressed from those characteristics of infancy, through those of latency and adolescence, and finally to those of adulthood."[8]

While Garland et al. describe the group as a whole eventually going through a familylike stage, Cook and Munce conceptualize the group in its entirety as a family setting in which members are helped to progress through their individual life stages. These perspectives complement each other.

6. *Development of Socializing Techniques*

One must have at least the most basic social skills in order to become and remain a member of a group, and as noted, the isolated, abusive, parent population is usually deficient in this area. However, whether it is the stated purpose of the group or a by-product of its processes, members can be helped to acquire or improve their interpersonal relationship skills as a result of their group experience.

If we accept the notion that social isolation is in and of itself a contributing factor to child abuse and neglect, then it becomes important to help the members gain the confidence and ability to develop a personally satisfying social existence. Behaviorists have demonstrated that behavioral change can occur without personal insights. Learning how to make and be a friend can go a long way in promoting healthy parental behavior, even without insight into the etiology of the problem.

7. *Imitative Behavior*

Whether through identification or reinforcement, or simply as a basic phenomenon of its own, we have all observed that individuals copy behaviors to which they have been exposed. This can happen with or without awareness. In the group situation members "try on" the behaviors and speech patterns of the other members and will tend to keep those behaviors that fit well or are consistent with their personal aspirations.

The Madison Avenue slogan, "Try it. You'll like it," could well be applied here. Because of the human tendency to imitate, the simple exposure to more successful and constructive ways of handling and coping with problems can bring about the incorporation of new and satisfying behavioral patterns.

8. *Interpersonal Learning*

Yalom divides this curative factor into three components. He elaborates upon: (1) the importance of interpersonal relationships, (2) the corrective emotional experience, and (3) the group as a social microcosm.

The first and third of these components have already been discussed. The second component, the corrective emotional experience, will be elaborated upon here.

Yalom quotes Franz Alexander, who wrote in 1946 that the basic principle of treatment is "to expose the patient, under more favorable circumstances, to emotional situations which he could not handle in the past. The patient, in order to be helped, must undergo a corrective emotional experience suitable to repair the traumatic influence of previous experience."[9] Yalom adds that this experience is more likely to occur in the group setting: "in the individual setting the corrective emotional experience, valuable as it is, may be more hard to come by because of the insularity and unreality of the patient-therapist relationship."[10]

We have observed many instances in which the nonnurturing parent has expressed and acted out with the group strong negative feelings about the significant others in his life or about fellow group members. As this individual is confronted with the impact of his behavior on his relationships with others and is helped to correct distorted perceptions of reality which may provoke the destructive behavior, new behaviors can be acquired.

9. *Group Cohesiveness*

Yalom writes: "By definition, cohesiveness refers to the attraction that members have for their group and for the other members. Members of cohesive groups are more accepting of each other, more supportive, more inclined to form meaningful relationships in the group. Cohesiveness seems to be a significant factor in successful group therapy outcome."[11]

In many ways, this factor is a prerequisite for the others. Unless one is attracted to a group and feels accepted by it, it is unlikely that the previously discussed factors will have an impact.

Cohesiveness relates to the degree of influence the group as a whole will have on any one of its members. Models of group-work practice vary in how much cohesion is encouraged. While fostering cohesion on the one hand, the worker must help the members maintain their individuality on the other. For example, in a discussion of whether or not to give up children for foster care, the worker must make sure that the group does not reach a decision to which all the members feel bound because of their commitment to the group as a whole. Foster care may be the answer for one group member and not for another. Cohesiveness should enhance the value of each individual's uniqueness and not eradicate or smother individual differences.

10. *Catharsis*

Yalom defines catharsis as "the expression of a strong emotion,"[12] and he expresses surprise that the patients in his survey rated it as an important curative factor. He also notes that it is rated highly more because of its positive effect on interpersonal relations than because of the simple relief of "getting things off one's chest."

We believe from our observations of group work with abusive parents that verbal expression of pent-up anger within the group setting significantly helps reduce the amount of hostility that gets acted out toward children. It is especially valuable for this release to occur in the presence of caring others so that the vacuum left by the emotional release can be filled with the concern these others express. In this way, the individual is not left with potentially destructive feelings of helplessness and emptiness.

Additional Contributions of Group Work

In addition to Yalom's ten curative factors of group treatment, there are three other special contributions that groups offer to their members. Although aspects of these overlap with factors already discussed, they are important enough to identify in their own right.

1. *The Opportunity to Hide*

While many people would naturally assume that an introverted or shy individual would adapt more quickly to casework rather than group-work treatment, it could also be argued that the opposite is true. Abusive parents fall anywhere on the introvert-extrovert continuum and such personality differences potentially enhance the group experience. In fact, Robert Paradise and Robert Daniels define a properly balanced group as one in which such differences exist. "Our own definition is that a balanced group is one in which tensions and differences exist so that movement and action may take place. An imbalanced group is one in which all members are predominantly the same." [13]

Reserved, cautious group members can test the safety of the group experience by observing more outspoken, risk-taking ones. Each exchange between the worker and one group member sends messages to all the other members about how the worker will react to them and on their behalf. In a one-to-one situation the client is on his own, and this may be very threatening to a passive, introverted person.

2. *Evoking Different Aspects of the Personality*

We all know that we behave somewhat differently with the various people in our lives. Some of our friends or family members are easier to talk seriously with and still others may bring out our sense of humor. While there exists an integrated central core, the variations in each person's personality cannot be denied. Several personality facets may be manifested in a relationship with any one person but even more emerge in relationships with many people. So it is in the group situation. The multiple relationships and interpersonal transactions within the group evoke many aspects of a single member's personality structure and these become accessible to interventions by the worker and other members. In this way, the "whole" person can be reached rather than the "partial" person that is revealed in a one-to-one relationship.

3. *Creating New Norms for Parental Behavior*

Most of our discussion so far has focused on the psychological aspects of treatment for child abuse and neglect. We have noted that most known cases of child abuse and neglect occur in a cultural environment that supports violence as a solution to problems. Child abusers are themselves often abused spouses or lovers. The stories they relate about their families and acquaintances often refer to violent acts. Violence toward children is an integral part of this social milieu.

In the group as a social microcosm the members themselves participate in the formulation of norms for parental behavior. The norms developed through peer interaction have a greater impact on an individual and are more easily incorporated than are those that are passed down from a professional. With success, new standards for interpersonal problem solving will place physical violence on the lowest rung of a hierarchial value system for human behavior, and this factor can serve as a deterrent to abuse.

Objections to Use of Groups

Historically, abusive parents have been and still are treated primarily through one-to-one professional intervention in spite of the many benefits of a group experience. In order to encourage the widespread use of groups, it is important to identify the factors that limit the creation of such opportunities for this client population.

The problems associated with group-work practice are not insurmountable. Several of them will be identified here and solutions will be elaborated upon in later chapters which describe and analyze actual group-treatment experiences with abusive mothers.

1. *The Nature of Professional Education*

Social work began as casework and this remains the most widely practiced social-work method. Most professionals have specialized in individual counseling and are understandably less comfortable offering group services. They may, in fact, lack group-work skills. If worker enthusiasm for running groups is perceived as a positive factor, then worker resistance as a negative factor must also be taken into account.

This problem can be overcome with the help and guidance a group-work consultant can offer. The principles of practice that underlie one-to-one intervention are applicable to group-work situations, and a consultant can be effective in helping practitioners make the transition. Since isolated people are especially difficult to serve through groups, it is important for workers to build in the supports they need to help them meet the challenges they will face. In addition to providing knowledge, which helps build confidence, the consultant can also provide support by sharing in decision-making with the worker about the best ways of handling the problems that arise.

2. *Concern about Confidentiality*

Protective workers frequently express concern that abusive parents will fear exposure in a group situation, but this may be more of a concern for the worker than for the client. The comforts of peer support usually outweigh the initial embarrassment of talking about problems in front of others. When prospective group members learn that they will be sharing an experience with people who are like themselves, they frequently feel the relief of the "universality" factor even before the first meeting. Those parents for whom confidentiality is a matter of true concern are free to reject group participation. Worry about confidentiality is not a valid reason to withhold a group-work opportunity from others.

3. *Practical Arrangements*

On a practical level workers face the frustration of arranging for transportation to a central meeting place and the difficulty of making arrangements for child care during meetings. These problems can be turned into advantages. Workers who personally transport members to and from meetings frequently find that informal discussions in the car become quite significant.

Child-care arrangements can also be arranged creatively. One protective agency provided a social worker as a leader for a children's play group that met while the mothers attended their meeting. Not only did the children receive a beneficial group experience, but the staff was also able to gain a greater understanding of the family situation through the social worker's observation of the children and their own observations of the parent-child interactions during drop-off and pick-up time. Eventually the mothers began to chat with the children's worker, much as most parents do with their children's caretakers, and yet another opportunity for professional intervention was created.

Workers must include planning for practical arrangements in the time required for group-work practice. These concrete services are obvious forms of giving and caring and provide additional opportunities for enhancing the therapeutic experience.

4. *Erratic Attendance Patterns*

Perhaps the most serious drawback in maintaining a group experience is the difficulty in getting the parents to attend meetings with any regularity. The worker is usually not nearly as upset when a client misses a one-on-one interview as he is when four out of six members do not show up for a meeting. Not only does this deal a blow to the worker's ego but it also results in the shared embarrassment of rejected feelings between the worker and the members in attendance.

The worker must not become discouraged by the exaggerated resistance to group membership that is found in this isolated population. Each meeting that a member attends is a success upon which an eventual commitment to the group can be built. As the group progresses through its developmental phases, attendance becomes more regular and, to some extent, the problem resolves itself.

In the following chapter, the principles discussed so far will be referred to in the description and analysis of group-work experiences designed to prevent and treat child abuse.

Chapter 4
Differential Group Work Evolves In A Protective Agency

This chapter describes the evolution of a successful group-work program in an agency that once provided treatment through the casework method alone. The agency's first group was based on what Catherine Papell and Beulah Rothman describe as the remedial model,[1] in which group work is focused on the intrapsychic dynamics of each individual. The explicit purpose of this model is to find solutions to personal problems, or as Fritz Redl says, to do "repair work." It is the approach that most closely resembles casework treatment and therefore the one caseworkers most often offer to their clients. The group-work program that ultimately developed in this agency offers additional group-work models for a variety of purposes and phases in the treatment of families.

Children's Protective Services is a private agency, located in Massachusetts, that provides social-work services to families referred because of child abuse or neglect. Founded in 1878, it has been known through the years as the Massachusetts Society for the Prevention of Cruelty to Children. It is the only private agency in the country whose central purpose is to provide protective services to families on a state-wide basis. It has twelve district offices throughout the state.

The agency views the family as a total unit that should remain intact except when a child's emotional or physical safety is in jeopardy. The service program provides intensive, in-depth service to its families, using the psychosocial diagnostic and treatment approach. Seeking new methods to help children and adults, the Boston District Office of Children's Protective Services (hereafter referred to as the agency) began in 1970 to use group-work practice.

Three separate models of social group work emerged through the years: (1) a remedial discussion group for mothers for the purpose of personal problem solving, which focused on the intrapsychic dynamics of each member; (2) a developmental activity group for the adolescent daughters of client families, focused on member interactions, for the purpose of helping them to accomplish psychosocial developmental tasks; and (3) a task-oriented group for parents in which therapy was linked to successful task completion.

27

A detailed description and analytical discussion of the first two models will be found in Chapters 5 – 7. The task-oriented group will be detailed later in this chapter.

Mothers' Remedial Discussion Group

The major goals of the remedial discussion group were to relieve the mothers' depression and sense of social isolation and to provide alternate ways of handling problems, such as child rearing skills, welfare and housing. Membership was limited to mothers whose backgrounds and problems were similar, and who were neither retarded, psychotic nor drug-addicted. The group formation process, which took several weeks, began with the caseworkers introducing the idea to clients they believed would benefit from the experience. If a woman indicated an interest, the group worker visited her in her home to further discuss the group purpose and format and to establish a beginning relationship. The weekly meetings were to last an hour and a half each, and the group would meet from fall to spring. The women were assured that the content of meetings would be confidential, and the importance of regular attendance was stressed. Transportation was provided by the workers and a special cab driver was paid by the agency for members who did not live on a reasonable pick-up route. The agency also provided baby-sitting services.

Of the thirteen women visited, ten joined. By midwinter three had dropped out, and weekly attendance ranged from three to seven mothers. Initially the members found it difficult to establish trust and to demonstrate concern for each other. A meeting marked by openness and candor would be followed by a session with high absenteeism, anger and distrust. Yet, by the time the group ended in the spring, the women were sharing their past and present problems and mutually exploring ways of coping with them. The women expressed sadness at the group's ending and spoke of the need for such a group for their adolescent daughters. The professional staff agreed that many of the treatment goals had been met, and they isolated two internal agency issues which they found infuenced group-work practice.

1. *Relationship Between Group Worker and Caseworker*

The original contract with the group provided that no information would be transmitted by the group worker to the caseworkers. Thus, unintentionally, the group meetings became a separate service instead of an integral part of a treatment approach. It became clear that the mothers were disclosing information vital to their overall treatment more fully at group meetings than during their one-to-one sessions. They used the group to express anger toward caseworkers, their remarks often reflecting ambivalence about their own dependency needs and dependent relationships. The group worker had inadvertently set herself up as the "good parent" who listened to complaints about the "bad, punitive parent." The caseworker still had the primary protective responsibility and assumed the limit-setting functions, while the group worker could remain divorced from the authoritative role and sometimes appeared to clients as supportive of their complaints. This intensified normal competitive feelings between two workers involved with the same client and subtly undermined the casework relationship.

The contract was modified after one mother had an abortion and told the group members and group worker but not her caseworker. Group members were informed that workers would share necessary information with each other, including the client in the process. The women did not object to this arrangement. After modifying the contract with clients on this issue, the agency moved closer to developing an integrated treatment approach.

2. *Worker Accountability*

The biweekly meetings of the group worker, and her supervisor were crucial in developing the group-work program. The support of the administrative staff was important to the leader, who at times felt no other staff members understood the stress she faced. It was also important for the administrative staff to learn the results of this treatment method in order to reinforce interest in additional group treatment plans. The conference tied what would otherwise have been an ancillary service to the overall agency program and helped to keep the worker highly motivated.

Need for Persistent, Consistent Outreach

Participation in the group was voluntary. Any mother who showed a desire to break out of isolation and become a group member was encouraged to do so. Clients who showed no interest were not urged to join. During visits to their homes, the mothers expressed positive feelings about joining the group, but the group worker still had to use outreach techniques to resolve ambivalent feelings. Garland et al. refer to the first phase of group development as the "approach-avoidance" stage.[2] They believe that all group members have a need to explore and test a situation before mutual trust and cohesiveness develops. The staff learned not to be discouraged by erratic attendance patterns and not to feel professionally threatened by the members' need to act out their fearfulness, anger and general insecurities in this way. Each absence was followed by letters, telephone calls, and if necessary, a home visit. Thus, group members learned that others expected them to attend and that, in a sense, they were being asked to account for each absence. Each return to the group meetings won praise from the group worker, and eventually from the other women. As they came to realize that the group worker was serious in her concern for them, the mothers began to develop trust and become invested in the group.

Encouraged by this experience, the agency subsequently set up other groups that included women from the original group together with new referrals. The mothers' remedial discussion group had become an accepted treatment modality at the agency.

Adolescent Girls Group – A Socialization Group

After this success the agency hired a social group worker in order to expand its group-work program. The new worker and another took an intensive course in group work to help them plan a group for adolescents with themselves as co-leaders. The first meeting of this group occurred nearly two years after the mothers' group had begun.

Originally the goals were similar to those of the mothers' group, but distinct differences between the populations became clear during planning. The workers decided to add activities as a therapeutic tool, rather than relying primarily on dialogue, since verbalizing is often more difficult for adolescents than for adults. Also, the workers believed that, with the girls' emerging sexual feelings and energy, it would be almost impossible to contain them for an hour and a half of discussion. The workers recognized that the girls still had to master normal developmental tasks, including the acquisition of social skills, and were very aware that adolescents considered peers the "significant others" in their lives. The group was perceived as an entity in and of itself, with an existence and development that received as much attention as the behavior of any one member. Interaction, whether member-member or members-workers, was studied intensely. The theory behind this approach is that social development is most likely to occur in a healthy social environment, and since social development was a goal for the group members, the workers had to create that social environment. The wide range of activities – from crafts and bowling to eating and talking – was useful in attaining that end. Since group and individual growth and development were the foundation and purpose of the group, the authors refer to this as the developmental model.

Caseworkers referred girls aged 11 to 13 from their caseloads. The major criterion was that they were acting out sexually or were likely to do so. The group purpose was twofold: (1) treatment, since the girls had experienced abuse or neglect within their families and were suffering from emotional deficits, and (2) prevention, since most of the girls were likely to become mothers and, without direct intervention, were likely to rear their children the same way they had been reared.

Caseworkers referred children on whom other services, such as Big Sister or school guidance counselors, were not making an impact and who were among the more disturbed, acting-out children in their caseloads. The families of the girls had good relationships with their caseworkers and saw the agency in a positive light. Parents as well as daughters were interviewed, and all expressed enthusiasm about the adolescent group.

The group of eight girls was fairly homogenous. Most of them were scapegoats within their families and came from homes that had a pattern of child abuse and other problems, including delinquent behavior, incest, loss of one parent, alcoholism, and so on. They were from large families with five or six children; their family income levels ranged from middle class to that of welfare recipients; and their homes were within a five-mile radius of one another. During the early stages of the group, one member was placed in foster care through court action but continued as a group member.

During the summer, meetings lasting about two hours were held weekly. Picking up the girls and returning them home often took another hour and much of the therapeutic work was done during these drives. Each girl usually manipulated time alone with a group worker during the ride or at the meeting. Pick-ups were frustrating for the workers since the girls lived in different areas, attended different schools, and often were sleeping when the leaders arrived. Initially the workers had to help them dress, get breakfast, and the like, to enable them to attend. Whenever a member did not attend, the workers followed through with phone calls and personal notes.

At the first meeting the leaders raised the issue of confidentiality. From experience the workers know the importance of sharing information with the family caseworkers. Group members were told that the leaders would at times share information with the caseworkers but not with the members' parents, except for a serious problem such as pregnancy or illness. In such cases the workers would discuss the matter with the members before involving parents. At the second meeting the workers reviewed the earlier discussion and found that the approach was acceptable to the group members.

After several sessions it became obvious that the adolescents were responding to the group experience. They were investing in relationships with each other and the workers. They were using meetings to work through issues, especially their anger and hostility to a world that had maltreated them. Their behavior was frequently uncontrollable. The meetings were often difficult and painful, for members and workers alike. It took several months before progress could be measured.

Activities as a Therapeutic Tool

At the start of the group, it was difficult for the casework staff to recognize the therapeutic value of activities. They perceived activities as something the group workers did for "fun," and initially the group workers felt that their efforts were not being taken seriously by the caseworkers. Social workers often resist the use of activities in their practice. Ruth Middleman states:

> Most probably the groupworker himself is primarily a verbal human being as he interacts with others in the normal course of his life demands. As a person who is college educated and often postgraduate educated, he is probably proficient verbally. Many a social work student is jolted by the realization that communication with the people he intends to help often requires a marked simplification of his very language.[3]

It is an even greater jolt to stop relying primarily on language at any level and to work toward understanding nonverbal behaviors expressed in activities. Yet, as the groupworkers started interpreting at staff meetings what was happening within the group and consulting more frequently with the families' caseworkers, the diagnostic and therapeutic value of nonverbal communication was recognized and accepted, and activities were added to the repertoire of interventive tools.

Group Work Consultation

Workers from both the adolescent group and the mothers' group expressed their need for a group-work consultant, and one was hired for monthly sessions. The consultant supervised the group workers, met twice within the first six months with the full staff to discuss group-work theory, and helped staff identify and evaluate group-work modes.

The co-workers of the adolescent group made a report to both the district and statewide boards of directors describing and interpreting the group goals, process, content and results. The boards encouraged staff to expand the use of groups in the agency.

The Christmas Party Committee – A Task-Oriented Group

For years the staff had been organizing a Christmas party for all the families they served. Concerns about violating confidentiality by bringing clients face to face were dispelled as attendance at each year's party grew. When the group-work consultant suggested that the clients be involved in planning the party, the agency recognized the therapeutic potential of a task-oriented group. Such a group is described by Catherine Papell and Beulah Rothman as the "Social Goals Model":

> The model assumes that there is a unity between social action and individual and psychological health. Every individual is seen as potentially capable of some form of meaningful participation in the mainstream of society. Thus the Social Goals Model regards the individual as being in need of opportunity and assistance in revitalizing his drive toward others in a common cause and in converting self-

seeking into social contribution. The therapeutic implication of social participation makes the application of this model available to groupwork practice, with groups of varying illness and health.[4]

This task group was the first of its kind formed within the agency. The workers believed that the project would help improve the women's self images, with the party itself a visible proof of their capabilities. The task group would not threaten the more reserved women because it would provide an experience in which they could interact and form relationships around nonpersonal matters, rather than around their problems, and work with others in a structured situation toward a shared goal. With this in mind, workers referred several mothers they hoped and believed would gain enough confidence and comfort within a group to proceed to a more intense problem-oriented remedial discussion group. Since the task-group project was similar to a group experience any adult might have in the general community, it was also perceived as potentially helpful to mothers in the process of terminating from treatment. It could serve as a laboratory for normal adult functioning in the community at large. In this way, the task group evolved as a "halfway" experience to help clients move in and out of more formalized treatment groups.

The task group was composed of ten women ranging in age from their late 20's to mid 40's. The group met six times to plan the party and once afterward to celebrate its success. Committee members who had been in the mothers' discussion group were the first to assume leadership in the task group, perhaps reflecting the confidence gained from that experience.

Since this was a generally impulsive population, the co-leaders broke the planning process into smaller tasks that could be completed at each meeting or between meetings instead of leaving issues open-ended. Thus, members left each week with the sense of having accomplished something concrete. Their responsibilities included handling invitations, shopping for presents and soliciting others from downtown merchants, planning for and preparing food and arranging for entertainment.

Many secondary gains were achieved. For example, the member responsible for the invitations showed a heretofore undiscovered artistic talent in designing them. She also involved her husband and children in the project, although they had rarely done anything together. Another husband volunteered to be the party's Santa Claus and received positive recognition for a job well done.

The workers extended themselves as much as was required to help the members carry out their assignments. They contacted them between meetings to serve reminders and offer help if it was needed. Since many of the women had no telephone, contact frequently took the form of a written note and an occasional home visit. The task group could only be therapeutic if it broke the cycle of non-achievement the women had created for themselves.

As the task group met, the members became increasingly comfortable with each other and began using meetings to talk about personal issues, evidence that they were capable of utilizing group processes for personal growth. It was important for two reasons that the workers resist the temptation to permit the members to drift from their task into a personal-problem focus. First, it would be unethical to "trick" people into treatment if the verbalized working agreement between the members and the workers was to plan for a party. Second, if the experience was to prove ego-strengthening, the workers had to ensure a sense of achievement by protecting the members from failure to reach their goal. If the mothers had not planned and carried out a successful party, their images as nonachievers would have been reinforced. At the same time the workers directed the women back to the task, they encouraged them to join a discussion group that was going to begin after New Year's.

Another important factor in gratification was food. At first the leader provided coffee and doughnuts. As the group progressed, members made pastry and brought it to the meetings. (In the adolescent group, much food was consumed at dairy bars and pizza places.) The treatment value of food in working with groups merits major consideration.

The workers believed that committee participation had helped the members gain improved self-images and many were able to move into a discussion group. It also influenced the members' attitudes toward the agency which they had now served. In the past the server-recipient relationship had gone only in the other direction. Thus, a third model of group work was added to the agency program.

More Groups Evolve

The evolution of a group-work program is an ongoing process

within the agency. Perhaps the most important group-work principle learned is that professionals should think not only in terms of "Should this client be served in a group?" but also, "Which kind of group might serve this client best?"

As agency staff became more sensitive to the value of peer interaction, treatment potential was recognized in situations previously not considered in this light.

For example, preschool children of the women in various groups were placed for baby-sitting purposes in a group of their own. For most of these children this was their first experience away from home and their first opportunity for interaction with peers. Their behavior dramatically reflected their families' isolation and often chaotic living conditions. Through a case aide, a meaningful program to which the children responded was devised and the youngsters were helped with problems of separation and social functioning. Staff valued this nursery as therapeutic in itself. Formation of a group to include fathers is now being considered.

The agency's experience has proven that group participation enhances the quality of service to its client population. The very nature of protective services, as well as the needs of clients, requires that a wide variety of treatment opportunities be made available to families. Establishing a group and sustaining it in a protective setting requires a large investment of staff time. It does, however, add a unique and important dimension to the professional help given to clients. In many instances group work may supplement and have a positive effect on the casework process. In other instances it may be the treatment of choice and may replace the one-to-one intervention.

Chapter 5
Group Development And Grief Therapy: Description And Analysis Of The Mothers' Discussion Group

We have already asserted that abusive and neglectful parents are, on the whole, a difficult population to serve. Most have been referred or "reported" to a social-service agency and appear to enter into treatment with little motivation for behavioral change. They frequently speak of cooperating only out of fear that their youngster would otherwise be taken away. Workers often find these women demanding and generally hard to reach. Since many of the mothers are socially isolated and describe a pattern of poor interpersonal relationships, group treatment appears to be a particularly difficult challenge.

Yet, experience at the Children's Protective Services over a five-year period has shown group work to be an especially effective treatment modality for nonnurturing mothers. Within the discussion group, members achieved a recognition and understanding of inner feelings and life situations and discovered and developed inner strengths to cope with them. In this chapter the phases which characterized this movement will be described and analyzed in the light of group developmental theory. The workers' intervention will be highlighted in hopes that other professionals will feel encouraged to offer similar services and to add knowledge to the field.

The processes observed in these groups parallel those described in the literature on grief therapy. Denial, anger and depression preceded an ability to accept and cope with reality. As grieving for a missed childhood was an integral part of the treatment process, these parallels are understandable.

Bertha Simos writes:

> ...losses occur in psychotherapy through the giving up of neurotic patterns...of the childhood view of parents, of wishes and hopes unfulfilled, of missed experiences one will never have a chance at again...[1]

The depressed and acting-out group members needed to recognize and work through the grief of their own early deprivations before they could give up the destructive and self-defeating behavior that resulted from their attempts to compensate for their enormous emotional deficits. Their behavior reflected a never-ending search for a nonexistent idealized parent. Consequently, they had unreasonable expectations of acquaintances, authority figures and the people who played major roles in their lives.

Henry Grayson states:

> ...the depressed patient transfers that wish for maternal love to other maternal substitutes – spouse, friend, teacher, therapist, employer, and even government – expecting to find the perfect mother. When this hope is disappointed, the patient may flee in search of another and hopefully a more perfectly giving mother figure, or will become more demanding of the one(s) to whom he has attached himself.[2]

In the group, the women told of lovers and/or husbands who had in some way wronged or disappointed them, and of their own children who consistently challenged them and added to their difficulties and unhappiness. They looked to their children as an additional source of nurturance, rather than seeing them as the rightful recipients of parental giving.

Because the women tended to surround themselves with irresponsible and unstable people, there was an element of reasonableness in their many complaints about interpersonal relations. The women had little awareness, however, of their own role in forming and maintaining these unsatisfying relationships. They continually found a logic and justification for their expectations of others and for their own behavior. Only after realizing the hopelessness of their wish to become "cherished daughters" and mourning the abandonment of such an impossible hope were they free to develop new behaviors to cope with life as it existed and not life as they projected it to be.

Bertha Simos adds:

> "Mourning – the expression of grief, involves the specific psychological task of breaking the emotional tie with that which has been lost and eventually reinvesting one's attachment to living people and things."[3]

The grieving rituals of nearly every society offer mourners a supportive network of peers and relations. In the discussion group, members provided for each other the support system that existed nowhere else for them. The development of such group support for the emotionally and socially isolated individual is a crucial aspect of grief therapy.

Setting and Background

The agency's group-work program was developed to help the isolated clientele use peer relationships and community supports. It was also anticipated that their unsatisfactory relationship patterns would be re-enacted in the group and that their intrapsychic and interpersonal conflicts thus would be accessible for professional intervention.

All of the group members were originally receiving individual treatment and were referred to the group by their caseworkers. They were all neglectful or abusive parents and had themselves been neglected and abused children.

The Worker as a Group Participant

Although most discussions of group treatment focus on the client participants, the worker as a group member cannot be exempted from analysis. This is especially true when dealing with a needy population that makes excessive and provocative demands on the worker. For clients who suffer from severe parental deprivation, even the most subtle reactions of the worker, who is eventually viewed as a parent surrogate, take on an exaggerated importance. The worker capitalizes on the transference and subsequent countertransference phenomena in order to promote the "reparenting" process that is central to treatment.

When the worker can identify personal feelings and integrate them with professional knowledge, diagnostic acumen and interventive skills become enhanced. It is a frequently misconceived notion that professional discipline requires the worker to neutralize his or her personal emotional reactions. Professionalism requires setting aside only those feelings that would not further professional purposes. It does not exclude the use of feelings that can serve to deepen the human quality of the therapeutic experience. For this reason, the identification and utilization of the workers' feelings will be described as the group experience in its entirety is discussed.

Group Formation and Early Meetings

The stages of group development observed by the workers are consistent with those described by James Garland, Hubert Jones, and Ralph Kolodny. They are: (1) preaffiliation (approach-avoidance), (2) power and control, (3) intimacy, (4) differentiation, and (5) separation.

During the group-formation process, the group workers (a male and female) made many home visits to potential members in order to establish a relationship that provided each one with enough support to face the potential hazards of group membership. In this way the workers also served as a liaison between each member and the group as a whole.

Since individual roles in the group did not emerge at the early meetings (that happened during the second stage) and since "leader" is one of these roles, it was the workers' responsibility to fill the leadership vacuum. (As the group progressed and indigenous leaderhip emerged, the workers assumed other important roles. The group workers were not always the group leaders.) The workers began the first meeting by making clear and concise statements about the purpose of the group and its structure and format. The expressed purpose of the groups was to help the women better cope with child-rearing problems and to help relieve their feelings of isolation and depression. Members were invited to contribute to the development of the contract, but the workers did not hold back from moving the group forward, even though the members could not articulate their feelings and thoughts beyond saying that it would be nice to talk with other women. The statement of the group purpose provided a framework for the coming experience, helped to reduce the anxiety of the unknown, and provided a structure within which contributions to and modifications of the working agreement were made when the members became ready to do so.

At the first meeting the members introduced themselves and began to work at establishing a group identity. They talked with little or no emotion about where they lived, what schools their children attended, where they were brought up, and the important adult relationships in their lives. Problems were expressed in terms of what someone or some institution was or was not doing to make them miserable, but not in terms of their own behavior. When underlying affect did spill out, it was often out of proportion to the situation at hand, or expressed in terms of extreme concern for someone the member hardly knew. The superficiality with which they talked about themselves and their situations stemmed in part form the normal need at this stage for interpersonal distance, but it was also an expression of their own emotional distance from their inner feelings.

The workers felt impatient about the apparent lack of introspection and depth displayed during this early phase of group development. However, even seemingly insignificant subject matter and the intensity and direction of displayed feelings furnished good diagnostic clues about each member, providing a starting point for intervention. Premature limit setting on seemingly irrelevant subject matter could have blocked the natural flow into more personal material, which gradually occurred with encouragement from the workers. It could also have frightened away members who needed the intrapsychic and interpersonal distance at this point.

Interpersonal Conflict and Angry Feelings

After the first few meetings, individual member roles began to emerge. Competition, sometimes fierce, arose for the most desirable ones. If the group was to have a scapegoat (most groups do not have a full-fledged scapegoat), that role would have emerged at this point as well. The "politeness" and denial of true feelings that characterized the preaffiliation stage were replaced by the readily expressed irritability and anger that typify the power-and-control stage. Interpersonal conflicts developed between members, between members and workers, and between competitive subgroups.

Saul Bernstein states that for conflict to exist, it is essential "that there be a struggle over something that is scarce – there is not apparently enough to go around to satisfy the contending parties. The scarcity may apply to material resources, power, status, or values. Those involved ordinarily assume that what their opponents get they will lose, and vice versa."[5] The group members feared a scarcity of the workers' love and attention, and a loss of control over themselves and the others.

Although the emerging conflicts were painful for all, it was only through their successful resolution that individual and group maturation came about. Conflict provided the momentum for change and growth.

Though the rewards of membership in a cohesive group can be great, such an experience has its costs as well. By identifying with each other, the women gave up defenses that protected privacy. They became more vulnerable to emotional pain. The members sensed the potential losses, tested the situation for the safety it could afford, and jockeyed for a controlling or safe position. Members formed alliances or subgroups for added strength and protection. An example drawn from group meetings will illustrate how the workers intervened in situations in which these subgroups threatened the development of group cohesiveness and caused other members to suffer the pain of exclusion.

Two participants, Tessie and Sally, came in each week with titillating stories of their weekend partying. They appeared to have a pact about what would be shared or not shared and frequently spoke for each other. They successfully monopolized each meeting with entertaining stories of sexual acting-out. They appeared to be usurping the leadership role from the workers and other potential indigenous leaders. While initially the members enjoyed the jokes and the distance they provided from their own problems, they eventually became angry in their passive role as audience and about the lack of movement toward the primary reason for meeting – that is, help for each of them in coping with their own problems.

The workers sensed the tension created in the group by Tessie's and Sally's behavior. As the other women could not identify with Tessie's and Sally's experiences, and as Tessie and Sally resisted all attempts to use their stories as a bridge to broader-based goal-related material, the workers set limits on what had become disruptive behavior. They pointed out to Tessie and Sally that is seemed much easier for them to continue with stories about social acquaintances than to talk about issues related to their children and families and about their own feelings.

Tessie and to a lesser degree, Sally, reacted by angrily withdrawing from group interaction. Tessie got up to go to the ladies' room three times and opened the window to yell and whistle at a man working on the street below. At the following meeting she wore a short skirt and a button which read, "How about a quickie?" Seductive behavior toward the male worker was coupled with open hostility toward the female worker. She said she was angry enough at the female worker to "punch her out." It was as if Tessie were attempting to form a new and more powerful subgroup with the male worker, now that her subgroup with Sally had been "attacked." This behavior was consistent with what was known about Tessie's early childhood. She transferred these feelings to the group by perceiving the female worker as an attacker and the male worker as a potential ally.

Although the workers feared that Tessie was angry enough to drop out of the group, she continued to attend meetings and after a few weeks was finally able to discuss the incident. It was another member who confronted Tessie's distortions of what had happened and attempted to correct Tessie's misconceptions of the female worker's role. This member also supported the worker by sharing her own feelings of how Tessie's and Sally's behavior had made all the other members feel left out and angry. Tessie was now reasonable and rational and rejoined the group as an active and more appropriate participant.

Tessie had been permitted to experience a safe rebellion, one that ultimately was not destructive to her or others or destructive to the group process. She was allowed to express her anger in the group with her obvious attention-seeking behavior. She had never before been able to rebel without suffering retaliation. The workers accepted her angry feelings, continued to reach out to her and provided opportunities to enable her to return to the group. They did not, at this point, explicitly relate the incident to Tessie's over-all behavior patterns. That needed to wait until later.

As the workers' reaction to the anger was so different than anything previously experienced by the members, a normative crisis was created. That is, the members realized that the norms in this group were different from those in the rest of their lives. Even though Tessie was the central figure in this incident, the resolution of the conflict between her and the worker affected the group as a whole. Everyone learned how the workers would respond to deviant behavior. For that reason, this incident cannot be interpreted as disruptive to the group process. On the contrary, it served to reinforce group development. Incidents like these help the group members build to a turning point in the therapeutic process, from suspicion and alienation to mutual trust and greater intimacy.

During this stage, the struggle for power and control was frequently expressed in discussions about the relationships between the members and the agency. The members voiced ambivalence about their dependency on the agency and on their individual caseworkers by alternately complaining about agency intrusion and expressing gratitude for all they have received. Janice, for instance, preserved her feelings of being "in control" by implying that she could manipulate the worker. She told of throwing the worker out of her home, claiming to admit the worker only on her terms. She then went on to boast about all the things her worker had done for her.

The members vied for the largest share of the group workers' attentions by presenting themselves as the neediest in the group. The effect was reminiscent of the 1940's radio program "Can You Top This?". They told stories of past or present deprivation, violence, instability and abuse in a rote, singsong manner and without affect. For example, Sandra stated that her mother died when she was 5 or 6 and that before her death her mother was bedridden for many years. Sandra didn't know the cause of her mother's death, but she did remember climbing out of her yard to spend the day with a neighbor who washed and fed her. When she returned home, after many hours, her mother never missed her. Pat spoke of repeated beatings when her parents were drunk, including one time when her father tried to pound nails in her head. Meg told of being tied in the backyard day after day in the summer, while her oldest brother was allowed freedom of movement and playmates. The women often stated that they had thought everyone was treated the way they were.

The members further tested the workers by telling about the physical punishments they inflicted upon their own children. Maureen, who was giving her preadolescent daughter double messages about school attendance, announced that she had beaten the child with a baseball bat (later it emerged that the bat was plastic) when she learned the child was truant again. Initially, the other group members supported this striking out at children as a necessary way to gain control. The workers accepted and gave permission for the verbal expression of anger and frustration, but they also moved Maureen toward an understanding of what provoked her violent responses. Maureen was asked about how she was feeling the day she lost control over her daughter's truancy. She explained that her father was in the hospital and that she had not been able to visit him because she didn't have a ride. This led to Maureen's expression of annoyance at her mother who was pressuring her to visit and do things for her father. The worker asked if she felt that her mother made excessive demands on her. Maureen then disclosed a lifelong pattern of exaggerated parental demands and expectations she could never meet. The worker encouraged Maureen to identify the true target of her anger. Since anger was an easily accessible emotion at this stage in the group's life, Maureen was able to recognize and express her anger at her parents. Till then Maureen had not fully accepted her own anger at her parents, partly because she thought her parents behaved as all parents did.

This last point illustrates how group processes helped members to bring emotions to the surface. With group support and professional intervention previously displaced feelings were directed to their true target. Destructive acting-out toward imagined parental surrogates was recognized for what it was.

While these group dynamics were in evidence, the workers often felt frustrated by the aggressive, competitive and demanding behavior encountered in the group. Through understanding the source and purpose of the provocative behavior and why it provoked their anger, however, the workers remained able to accept the members without becoming punitive in return. They remained strong and in the present, reacting with appropriate social responses which included a recognition of the feelings evoked in themselves and in the members but excluded even the most subtle rejections.

Trust, Grieving and Reparenting

When the members no longer feared a scarcity of the workers' love and concern and finally believed that the workers would not favor any one of them to the detriment of others, the conflicts of the power-and-control stage abated. Mutual trust began to flourish. The members no longer represented a threat to each other, but became mutual supporters instead. Fear of closeness diminished and the members began to identify with the workers' accepting and supportive posture, and with each others' sadly similar situations. The group had become greater than the total of what each of its members could individually offer.

It was during this, the intimacy stage, that the group members felt the workers to be caring and accepting parents and the fellow members to be supportive siblings. Though competition in the form of "sibling rivalry" still existed, it did not have its previous cut-throat quality.

The concrete signs of the intimacy stage included steadier attendance, a desire to close membership to new individuals, and a wish to continue with the group and extend it beyond the previously agreed termination date. The members displayed a genuine liking for each other and exhibited a mutual toleration of each other's most annoying characteristics. Emotions other than anger came more readily to the surface; tears and laughter were easily evoked. Whereas earlier the members had spoken with anger about all the "others" who were unfair and unjust to them, they now spoke with more appropriate affect about how their childhoods had affected them. Depression and sadness replaced anger as the overriding emotion of this developmental stage.

Before behavior changes could occur, the women needed to vent their anger, face their underlying depression, and mourn their lack of nurturance in childhood. Henry Grayson writes: "The patient must be helped to break through his denial to face the reality of missed experience or the impossibility of fulfilling infantile wishes. With both, decathexis takes place through the emotionally charged cathartic mourning, combined with the development of insight. Then...the person can move to collecting new objects and more realistic hopes."[6] The workers continually helped the members move toward being in touch with the terrible sadness that underlay the more easily expressed anger.

Weeks after Maureen was able to vent her anger at her parents for their unreasonable expectations of her, she was encouraged to feel and express her sadness at never having been nurtured in her childhood. She was given permission to feel sorry for herself, and the other members shared her sadness with her. Together they grieved for each other and themselves. It was often difficult for them to draw the line between crying for themselves and for each other. It was also unnecessary.

Kathy's mother was a prostitute. Most of the time she was in a barroom. When she did come home, she had a man with her. As a teenager, Kathy had to fight off the sexual advances of her mother's friend. Growing up, Kathy always had the responsibility for her younger brother. The only thing Kathy ever really wanted, but never got, was someone to love who would care for and about her. She always picked the "losers," and in the process ended up alone with six children. At times her pain and sadness overwhelmed and immobilized her. When the group reached the intimacy stage, she became a strong expressive leader who attended to the troubles and feelings of others. She began expressing her pain by writing poetry and sharing it with the other members. In the process, she and they became more aware of their needs and longings.

The professionals recognized the cost and risk to the individuals being encouraged to go through this painful process. Maintaining anger warded off responsibility to change. It was easier to exist in a world where others were responsible for all the wrongdoing. In addition, maintaining the anger helped to avoid the pain of feeling unloved – a pain that was harder to bear than the anger. For with the acceptance of being unloved came the feelings of worthlessness and undeservingness, and the guilt about the imagined misdeeds that merited such serious and profound rejection. It was the fear of facing this "emptiness" and guilt that kept alive the futile search for the all-loving good parent. Emotional self-revelation during intimacy did not lead to "emptiness," however, but instead opened the way for nourishment from the caring that the members extended to each other. The consistently accepting workers fostered a milieu in which it was safe to be vulnerable and in which there was relief from what might otherwise have been intolerable pain.

It was during this stage that the workers became more aware of their genuine affection for the members of the group. The counter-transference brought with it an empathy and feeling that went beyond the earlier felt professional concern for all clients in general. The workers did not hide their feelings from the members and sometimes responded to a particularly moving story with a simple touch on the shoulder. When a member once suggested that the workers could not possibly understand the sadness of her painful childhood, one worker responded by saying, "It is hard for me to understand, but I'm trying to, and you're helping me." Honest and open communication flowed freely and the workers took the lead in establishing and maintaining this momentum. The members felt the workers' genuine concern and accepted nurturing from them.

Several months after the limit-setting incident involving Tessie and Sally, Tessie observed a particularly moving exchange between the workers and a member. After a few moments of silence, Tessie thoughtfully volunteered to the workers, "You people are doing this for more than just the money. You've got to really care about us to put up with all you do."

Tessie now believed the workers did care, and with their help she and the other members were ready to begin again the process of emotional maturation that had been stifled years ago in their "first" childhood.

Behavioral Changes

Just as a child outgrows the need for intimate relationships within the primary family, the group members after many months (anywhere from twelve to fourteen months in these particular groups) began to move away from the intense closeness of the group ties. The members no longer saw each other as surrogate siblings but rather as women sharing an important and meaningful group experience with each other. The workers were no longer seen as "parents" but as caring professionals. The conversations began to turn to the everyday happenings of family life; only now that the members had accepted the truths of the past, the workers were able to help them focus on behavioral changes in coping with the stresses and strains of the present. It was during this stage of differentiation that the workers reviewed with Tessie how she had earlier perceived the female worker's limit setting as an attack. The group members were now less emotional, and they perceived behavior less symbolically and more realistically. By accepting the truths of their earlier lives, the members no longer assigned old meaning from a past life to present occurrences in new and different contexts. New-found personal strengths translated into new behaviors and responses.

After some time, Kathy began to try out at home the limit-setting techniques that were being discussed at group meetings. When her teenage son noticed a growing consistency in her responses to him, he remarked, "What's the matter with you? You going through the change?" She responded with, "Yeah, I'm finally growing up!" All the members shared Kathy' pride in herself.

Relationship of Group Development to Grief Therapy

Theories on grief therapy agree in their description of the progression of feelings and coping mechanisms in the handling of loss – whether of a loved one or in facing one's own impending death. Elisabeth Kubler-Ross describes the feelings during griefwork in the following order: denial of the reality, anger at its cruelty, depression and guilt for wrongdoings that deserve such punishment, and finally acceptance and coping.[7] These feelings and the order of their emergence are consistent with the group experiences already described.

Kubler-Ross describes the first stage of dealing with (impending) loss as denial of the enormity of the situation. While her patients sometimes refused to accept the facts of reality, our clients tended to show more of an affective rather than a cognitive denial. In the early meetings the mothers were aware of their own difficult situations and childhood, but narrated their stories with an emotional denial of the impact their histories were having on their present lives. When the group members did begin to show feelings, anger was the most accessible emotion. As the group reached the power-and-control stage, angry outbursts replaced emotionless monologues. Feelings of anger were expressed in their relationships with each other and on occasion with the workers, as well as toward the terrible other people in their lives. The mothers, too, were angry about the injustices of an unfair world. Kubler-Ross describes the mourner as moving from anger on to depression – depression about the reality of the loss. As relationships in the group survived the onslaught of the angry and testing meetings, the interpersonal relationships became stronger, and as the anger was spent, the group environment provided the safety needed for members to at last be in touch with their own depressed feelings. Without the group supports, this depression could have been annihilating. Kubler-Ross describes the final stage of mourning as acceptance of and preparation for impending death. Unlike the population with whom Kubler-Ross works, however, these clients became prepared for acceptance of life.

Chapter 6
Group Work For Outreach: Preventing Child Abuse

Most treatment groups for adults are focused on the discussion of personal problems and ways to cope with them. The success of this format is predicated upon at least two important conditions: (1) that group members are ready and willing to work on resolving problems they have identified and admit to having, and (2) that group members are at ease with verbal self-expression. When these conditions do not exist, professionals must find other ways to reach people they perceive as needing group services.

The developmental and socialization group, described in Chapter 4 as a group for adolescents, is one such alternative approach. This group-work model focuses on personal interactions within a context that resembles a microcosm of the broader social environment. Activities are an integral part of the experience since life itself is made up of thinking, talking and doing. This real-life quality is a major curative factor.

The following discussion describes and analyzes the use of the socialization model for preventive outreach.

Background and Setting

The Crittenton Hastings House of the Florence Crittenton Division of the Child Welfare League of America, an agency in Boston serving women with unplanned pregnancies, wished to extend its services to isolated, low-income, unmarried mothers (not necessarily pregnant at the time) who were not receiving any other social services. It was anticipated that such women would feel stress from their situation and it was feared that many of them were nonnurturing mothers, especially those with newborn infants. Gerald Hass states: "The isolated mother, who also may be severely depressed, may find these weeks intolerable. Without help or anticipatory guidance she may fall apart and present a high potential for child abuse or even infanticide."[1] The agency selected an inner-city public housing project to find potential members who could benefit from a group-work experience. The purpose of the group was to help members improve their parenting skills and to raise the level of their social functioning.

50

The social group worker assigned to this project began by planning the general format. Since she was trying to engage people who had never asked for help or presented a problem, she believed it would be unfruitful to organize a problem-oriented discussion group. She assumed that the prospect of attending such a group would be particularly threatening to women whose lifestyle did not include self-examining, psychologically oriented conversations with close friends. Instead she believed the women would probably be most in touch with and eager to address the boredom and loneliness in their lives. In order for the women to feel more comfortable, she wanted an approach that would permit them to maintain interpersonal distances until they felt safe within the group environment. She also believed the members would benefit from first relating around their strengths rather than their weaknesses. For all of these reasons, the social worker planned to integrate activities and discussion as the content of the group.

The next major issue was how to explain the group to the potential members. Although this was to be an activity group, it was important that the members not confuse it with a purely recreational experience. Julianne Wayne and Barbara Feinstein write: "It is a matter of professional ethics and good technique not to present an activity group as only that, unless recreation is indeed the primary goal...Unless the worker's true goals are verbalized as part of the working agreement, the worker has no sanction for directing conversation toward personal issues. Otherwise, this would be a seduction into therapy which is surely no worker's intent."[2]

Another consideration in approaching the women was their expected resistance to group participation since they were to be selected purposely because of their avoidance of social situations. They would surely wonder why they had been chosen and might be frightened or even affronted that professionals should feel the need to intrude upon their lives. In order to break through their resistance without avoiding truth, it was necessary to discuss the group in terms that reflected the members' rather than the worker's view of their needs. Instead of directly saying that the purpose of the group was to prevent child abuse and neglect, the group would be presented as a vehicle for relieving the stress of being a single parent and for finding ways to cope with the situation. The former approach is threatening and even accusatory. The latter holds promise of much-needed support.

The activities would be described as a means of relaxing and getting acquainted with others in a comfortable atmosphere. If the women preferred just to talk with each other about themselves and their lives, they would know that this was appropriate as well. Thus, the activities would not be presented as the group's aim, but rather as a means of reaching that goal. Most importantly, the women's needs would be expressed in the more neutral terms of their general situation rather than in terms of assumed shortcomings.

Finding Members and Forming the Group

The social worker began the group formation process by contacting the social-service staff of the health center situated in the housing project. Gerald Hass states: "Because the Neighborhood Health Center is situated where people live, it is well placed to be the most effective early warning system for identification and subsequent intervention in sociomedical problems. In retrospective examination of tragedies that we have all seen on hospital emergency floors, it becomes painfully obvious that many problems were predictable and that cries for help from families were not heard or, if heard, not understood."[3]

Since the social worker was interested in finding the most isolated women, the social-service staff suggested she meet with the Visiting Nurses who had contact with women who never even ventured into the health center and who spent most of their time alone in their apartments with their children. The social worker discussed her plans with the nurses and the nurses enthusiastically agreed that such a service was very much needed. The social worker asked for referrals of single women in their 20's with young children. She wanted women who were not retarded, psychotic or drug addicted. Heavy drinkers, however, were not excluded. She sought women with impaired social functioning – that is, with no known employment, friends, special interests or important stable relationships – women for whom the Visiting Nurses were the only ongoing professional contact.

The nurses were adept at selecting appropriate women for the group. They chose mothers whose children received no medical attention except from the Visiting Nurses, who were not fed appropriate diets and who spent too much time in soiled diapers and general uncleanliness. While there were no signs of serious abuse, hard spankings were the routine consequences of "bad behavior."

When the social worker agreed with their choice, the nurses discussed the possibility of group participation with the prospective member. The social worker was then brought to be introduced to those women who voiced enthusiasm about joining. The nurse did not usually remain for the entire interview. In all, six women – three black, one Hispanic, and two white – told the nurses they were interested. The social worker presented the group to them as she had planned. When she had explained that the meetings could be used as the women chose, for activities or just talking over coffee, each woman invariably picked up on the activity aspect. One woman said she had always wanted to learn to knit. Another said she had frequently watched bowling on television but had never gone and wondered if that was possible. Still another said she had not been to a movie theater in years and hoped the group could sometime go. The worker assured everyone that all of these suggestions were good ones and were all possible to do. It appeared to the worker that the women were eager to participate.

The worker explained the practical arrangements. She would personally provide transportation to the meeting place each week from a central meeting place yards from their apartment houses. Since no other facilities were available, the meetings were going to be held at Crittenton Hastings and the young pregnant women in residence would provide volunteer baby-sitting service. (Since many of the pregnant adolescents had never cared for young children, the staff believed it was a good opportunity for them to be exposed to other aspects of child care besides the sweet smell of baby powder. A social worker at the home worked with them and discussed the child-care experience with them each week.) The meetings would begin shortly and the group would continue to meet for an eight-month period. The time allotment was based on the worker's schedule and not on any known therapeutic formula.

By the end of the home visit, five of the six mothers said they wanted to join the group. One painfully shy woman could barely face the worker and said she was too busy to join right now. The other five agreed to be at the pick-up spot at the appointed time the following week.

While driving a van to the pick-up spot the day of the first meeting, the worker could not help but congratulate herself on her success.

This was supposedly a hard-to-reach population and, after only one home visit, five women had committed themselves to the experience. The self-congratulations were short-lived because, after waiting a half hour beyond the appointed time, the worker concluded that no one was going to show up. Recognizing that outreach meant just that, she returned to each mother's apartment and found each of them surprised to see her and in varying degrees of unreadiness to venture forth to a meeting. The worker insisted that the meeting was still going to be held. In one case she told a mother to get dressed while she diapered a toddler in need. Finally, two hours later than planned, four of the five original mothers and their eight children, ranging in age from ten weeks to four years, left the housing project for the first meeting.

The First Meeting

As the worker had anticipated, the women were very shy and awkward with each other at the first meeting. There was practically no eye contact between them. The car ride to the meeting was largely silent with a few tentative attempts at small talk. The women asked each other such things as how long they had been living in the project and the ages of their children. After leaving the children with the babysitters, the group went to their meeting place, a comfortable room with overstuffed chairs and couches, flowered curtains and a table with craft materials set in the middle. The worker began the meeting by reminding everyone of the purpose of the group: to relieve the pressures of being a single parent with children and to help find ways to cope with the stresses. She described the activities as a tool to help them feel relaxed and become acquainted with each other.

The worker tried to ease the members' anxieties by actively filling the leadership vacuum. She planned the activity for the first meeting, which was to make plastic flowers by dipping flexible wires into liquid plastic. Once the women began the project, the atmosphere became much more relaxed. The women could hide behind their activity and related more comfortably to their materials than to each other. As each of their flowers began to take shape, they became visibly proud of their achievements. These were not women who took creative achievement for granted. They did not have a history of such past successes. As children, they had not belonged to Girl Scouts or after-school special interest groups. This new experience was exciting for them and they eagerly shared their successes with each other.

As the women were working, the worker tried to help the members know each other better by guiding the conversation toward some personal but nonthreatening material. She told the group about an article in a popular women's magazine that attempted to analyze personality traits through favorite colors. The article stated that a preference for yellow indicated a strongly spiritual nature, while powder blue meant a strong desire for material luxuries. The women responded to this and easily began discussing their own color preferences and relating them to the personality traits they perceived in themselves. The conversation was light and fun and helped the mothers begin to share with and know each other.

The two-hour meeting ended with coffee and cake and the women agreed that the meeting had been enjoyable and that the time had flown. They gathered their plastic bouquets, cheerfully greeted their children and piled into the van to be driven home. They all agreed to be at the central pick-up spot the following week.

Subsequent Meetings

Still glowing with the confidence of their first meeting's success, the worker drove to the pick-up point the following week. Once again she was the only one to appear. As before, she returned to each mother's apartment, and relived the scenes of the previous week. Again the women offered explanations of why they would be unable to attend and again the worker asserted that they could attend and helped them to get ready.

This pattern of successful meetings followed by "no-shows" at the pick-up point continued, so after a few weeks the worker arranged to go directly to each mother's apartment. Eventually the women began to be ready for her arrival and three to four women of the five attended each meeting. Two women came nearly every week and the others attended with some irregularity. The worker contacted members between meetings if they had not been at home on the meeting day. For those without telephones, this meant writing a short note reminding them of the upcoming session.

With time, group cohesion grew and the women slowly became more comfortable and verbal with each other. The worker invited suggestions about the weekly activities and the women began to volunteer their ideas. The importance of varying the activities in order to build on their various abilities became clear when one particularly unartistic member achieved the highest score at the bowling alley. Although the crafts activities were noncompetitive in nature, this woman was aware that her work was usually sloppier and less pretty than the other women's. After her success at the bowling alley, which was recognized and commented upon by everyone, she felt so good and expansive that this usually timid person stopped at the refreshment concession and insisted upon buying treats for everyone, including the children and the worker. This particular successful moment would have been missed had the only group activity been crafts.

Although much of the group activity was nonverbal in nature, the worker looked for opportunities to encourage group discussion. Ruth Middleman writes: "The ideal program experience for any group would include both the verbal and the non-verbal means of expression, primarily because this is the true order of living itself. People express themselves through words and actions and the group experience should reflect this same balance."[4]

After the first few months, one of the women asked at the start of the meeting, "Is it all right if I just sit and talk today? I don't feel like working." The worker assured her that that was fine since the purpose of the group included having the opportunity to "just talk." At this point the other women had also begun to work less intensely on their project and to relate more to each other and the subject matter which was becoming increasingly personal. They were now talking about their problems, fears and hopes for the future. The group appeared to have reached what Garland, Jones and Kolodny consider the third stage of group development, intimacy. During this stage the members experience greater personal involvement and openness. "There is growing awareness and mutual recognition of the significance of the group experience in terms of personality growth and change."[5]

When possible, the worker guided their conversation toward child-rearing issues and the women began to ask for and give to each other advice about parenting. The worker stimulated them to think about their actions and sometimes challenged ideas they had come to accept. For example, Jenny told the group she did not believe in sterilizing bottles for her newborn or being what she considered overly concerned about cleanliness in general, because otherwise her child would not develop resistance to germs. Earlier a Visiting Nurse had expressed concern to the worker about this very attitude of Jenny's. The worker pointed out to her that she was running the risk of her daughter getting a serious infection before she had developed the resistances she needed. Betty said she wished Jenny's theory was true because life would be easier without the extra work. The worker said everyone sometimes tried to believe things they were not sure were true if those beliefs made life more pleasant. She added this was easier to do when the results were not immediately obvious. Marion said, "Like when I tell myself that smoking won't really hurt me." The women quickly launched into a discussion of self-deception through wishful thinking that left Jenny less comfortable with the rationale she had stated earlier. Once she no longer had the intellectual defense to support her behavior, an opening developed for the worker and the group to influence behavioral change.

Middleman also says: "Non-verbal content to be most effective has intermittent periods of verbal exchange and interpretation running throughout the experience."[6] The members' readiness for this type of exchange was demonstrated in the following incident.

About halfway through the group experience, Lena was at the point of antiquing a decoupage plaque she was creating. She was a particularly talented young woman and properly set about chipping its surface by banging it with a metal chain. After the first few tentative strokes, she began to hit it hard and with feeling. The worker recognized this and stated matter-of-factly, "You look angry." This remark triggered a spontaneous conversation among the women of the various ways they each handled their angry feelings. Lena said that when she became angry she ended up hurting herself. She gave as an example the last argument she had had with her boy friend. In order to punish him, she ordered him to leave her apartment although she actually preferred being with him. After he had left, she felt she had really only hurt herself. The worker knew there was significance to this personal revelation but did not know further what to do with the information at the time. The moment registered in her memory.

Several weeks later, after a discussion of the unplanned pregnancies they had all experienced, the worker suggested bringing in a film on birth control. All of the women were eager to see it except for Lena who remarked with irritation that everyone was alway trying to get her to use birth-control methods. She described how, after each delivery, the hospital staff tried to educate her accordingly. She said she was so annoyed at them for "pushing her" that she refused to listen. It was at this point that the worker confronted Lena with her own words: "You mean, Lena, that when you are angry you end up hurting yourself." Lena was visibly affected by this connection between her words and her actions. She was silent and thoughtful for the rest of the meeting.

About two months later, Lena announced to the group that she was pregnant but planned to have an abortion. She was then going to enter into a state-sponsored vocational program to which she had been accepted earlier. She was anxious to train to become a practical nurse. The other women were excited for her and supported her plans in spite of their earlier agreement that abortion was a terrible thing. Although the worker was pleased with Lena's plans and felt that they represented movement toward taking responsibility for her own life, she was concerned about the speed with which Lena had changed an entire value system. Rather than unabashedly supporting the decision, she encouraged Lena to think and talk about the sense of loss that would accompany her feelings of relief after the abortion.

The women then spoke seriously and with feeling about their children, about their love for them and the simultaneous grief for their own lost youth, for having themselves been what we today call "children with children." Lena did go ahead with her abortion, but she did so more prepared to cope with the painful aspects of such a choice.

Discussion

In retrospect, this group was viewed as a success by everyone connected with it, staff and members alike. During the experience, however, there was controversy among the professionals about aspects of the worker's approach. There were those workers who believed the group worker was being inappropriately aggressive with the members. These workers believed that if the women could not get to the pick-up point, then they did not really want or were not ready for the experience. In contrast, the group worker believed that the women's inability to follow through with a commitment was part of the very reason they had been recruited for group membership. The group worker viewed this behavior as a symptom of the larger problem being treated in the group. The group worker believed that getting the members to the group was as much a part of group work as anything that happened at the meetings. She thought it would be punitive to consider their not showing up as a lack of motivation that warranted a discontinuation of service.

The worker's aggressiveness had its effect. By the latter half of the group experience, the members began to phone the worker in advance if they were going to miss a meeting. When a social worker at the health center learned of this, she remarked, "Phoning ahead that you are not coming is as good as coming." What she meant by this was that the women had reached the point of feeling committed, responsible, and perhaps more importantly, that their absence would be felt. They had lost their sense of anonymity and knew they would be missed.

At the conclusion of the group, Lena did make plans for child care and enrolled in a vocational program. Another member found a job as an office clerk, and, while the other three women made no serious changes in their lives, they spoke of seeking other groups at the "Y" or local settlement house. The nurses, who continued their home visiting throughout the experience, reported that the women were becoming more attentive to their children and appeared to be trying out the new approaches to parenting that had been discussed over time in the group. They even began to use the health center for themselves as well as their children. The group experience had broken through their isolation and had helped them to move into the world around them, a world with people who could provide the emotional support to help them not hurt their children.

Chapter 7

Mixing Models: Activities as a Tool For Group Termination

This chapter will contain a description and analysis of a discussion-group experience in which activities were introduced to maximize the therapeutic value of the termination process. Although "discussion" and "activities" were described earlier as separate kinds of group experiences, it is also true that the selective use of each within the same group can help individual members and the group as a whole accomplish their respective goals and developmental tasks. Through the use of activities during the termination phase of a long-term remedial discussion group, a worker was able to help members use the ending of therapy as the beginning of a more normal socialization period. She was also able to minimize the regression that usually occurs during this difficult stage of treatment.

The experience to be described is that of a group of mothers being served by the Boston District Office of Children's Protective Services. The group was composed of women similar to others chosen for participation in discussion groups.

Group Termination

After thirteen months of weekly sessions, the worker observed that the women had progressed through the stages described in Chapter 5. They were now far less depressed than before and no longer seriously abusive or neglectful toward their children. As the group moved into the differentiation stage, meetings became less intense and less emotionally laden. During the differentiation stage the transference issues become largely resolved, and the members have a greater reality orientation.[1] As the women incorporated strengths, their dependency on each other appeared to be lessening. On one level, there seemed to be a natural "moving away" from each other, almost as if they had already given each other most of what they could at this point in their lives. On another level, however, they enjoyed their meetings very much and had developed meaningful friendships with each other.

It was at this point that the worker decided to set a termination date for the group. This was a difficult decision to reach because it was obvious that though the members had each improved noticeably, there were still gains to be made from staying together. However, given that there were limited agency resources and other clients needing services, a termination date was planned. The group was to meet for another three months; it would have been sixteen months by the time of its conclusion.

The worker was keenly aware of the potential effect of the termination process. Irvin Yalom stated:

> Termination is more than an act signifying the end of therapy; it is an integral part of the process of therapy; and, if properly understood and managed may be an important force in the investigation of change.

He goes on to say:

> The end of a group is a real loss; patients gradually come to realize that it can never be recovered, that even if they continue a relationship with a member or a fragment of the group, nevertheless the entire group will be gone forever. It is entirely analogous to the death of a loved one and may evoke memories of past losses.[3]

For this population, memories of past losses would evoke feelings that might well be expressed through an awakening of destructive violence directed toward their children. The worker wanted to minimize regression and use the termination process to help the members incorporate and stabilize the many gains they had made. She also wanted to provide experiences within the group situation that would encourage the development of behavior appropriate for the more normal life situations that exist outside of a therapy group.

It is helpful to consider the termination phase as having separate stages. Margaret Hartford described it in three parts:

> Pretermination or the plan of preparation for the actual ending; the termination itself – the recognized ending; and post-termination, the plan for follow-up, if any, of the group and the service.[4]

The worker began to plan for this phase even before announcing the termination date to the members. She wanted to foster the growing independence she had observed and wanted to increase the members' ability to relate to each other around the healthier aspects of their functioning. These women did not have many of the social skills needed to form and maintain friendships, and the development of these would certainly be an extension of the treatment plan. Thus the pretermination phase was designed to prepare members for posttermination situations.

Helen Northen described the worker's intervention during termination in the following manner:

> The social worker engages the members in discussions and action-oriented experiences to help them stablize the changes they have made. These activities are a natural progression from those in the preceding phase of development. They tend to be oriented to the community, such as ... participation in sophisticated social experiences that test the members' capacities for adaptive behavior.[5]

With this orientation in mind, the worker tried to plan group situations that would resemble community and neighborhood group experiences. She wanted to use the therapeutic potential of recreationally oriented and creative activities as a means of reaching this goal.

The worker began the termination process by encouraging a discussion in which the women were able to recognize and verbalize the progress they had made. Since the members felt so much more capable of coping with their problems than they did before, the worker suggested that their need for the group had lessened. She told them they could plan on staying together for another three months but that the group would be terminated after that. She also shared with them her perception that they enjoyed the social aspects of their meetings very much and suggested that they capitalize on this in their remaining time together.

The women were saddened to think of the group coming to an end but were responsive to the notion of using their meetings for more social purposes than they had before. They liked the thought of adding activities to their meetings while planning to continue with the discussions that held so much meaning for them. Together with the worker, they made plans for future meetings.

Thus, instead of the pretermination phase becoming focused entirely on "ending", the members were able to consider this a period of a new beginning.

At subsequent meetings, those members who had special creative skills taught the others, including the worker. The women especially enjoyed demonstrating skills that the worker did not have. This role reversal was satisfying to them and reinforced their growing feelings of mastery and independence. They clearly had become contributing members within the group situation. This was a far cry from their previous feelings of needing to be the recipient in their relationships with others.

The worker encouraged the members' emotional movement away from each other by introducing individually oriented craft activities, rather than those requiring group cooperation and effort. These craft activities included making paper flowers, Christmas wreaths, and wall hangings. As the women invested in what they were creating, they began to relate more to their materials and less to each other. They were visibly pleased with their newly developing form of self-expression. The members worked independently, but thoroughly enjoyed conversing with each other. The focus of their talk moved from their past deprivations to present pleasantries. Their humor changed from pathos to occasional lighthearted silliness. It was as if the enjoyment of the activities and the atmosphere created by them gave them permission and encouragement to identify the parts of their difficult lives that were acceptable and gratifying.

As their self-confidence grew and self-images changed, they spoke of new roles they perceived for themselves in the community. Three women gained part-time employment. One woman, who had previously talked of her church as a place to go for confession of wrong-doings and for food money, was now looking forward to donating to the church an art object she was creating at home. Another woman looked forward to joining a bowling league, and did, in fact, appear on a local television game show and bowled for a small cash prize.

Many of the dynamics of the termination process were acted out and resolved symbolically through the transactions involved in the crafts. By providing materials, the worker was able to meet dependency needs, giving something tangible while withdrawing as a therapist. She was also able to help members master skills that were immediately obvious to all. The need to be dependent was replaced with the pride of achievement.

One woman demonstrated regression by becoming angry and frustrated about her inability to add detail satisfactorily to a jewelry box she was making. In anger she almost completely ruined what she had done. The worker was able to help her repair the jewelry box while discussing how it was possible to misdirect angry feelings and make a situation even worse. The woman could make connections between that notion and her general behavior. Acting out the regression and increased dependency around her crafts activity reduced her need to regress in a more serious and irreversible aspect of her life.

Termination

The final meeting was a potluck luncheon suggested by the worker and planned by the members. This event was analogous to societal rituals which signal endings and transitions. This act of social sharing was symbolic of much that had transpired in the group. Each member showed ambivalence about exposing cooking talents, praised each others' specialties and shared her favorite recipes. The women expressed sadness that something that meant so much was ending, but they looked to the future in hopes of building on their new-found strengths. They also spoke of keeping in touch with each other. The worker helped them accept the loss of the group but also pointed out that they were each taking some special meaning from this experience which would become a permanent part of their being.

Posttermination

The worker had no plans to directly follow up on the outcome of group treatment. Many of the members continued in treatment with a caseworker from the agency, and this served as an indirect way of assessing the members' ability to sustain ego growth and the constructive roles they had assumed in their families and communities. Informal follow-up grew out of one member's part-time job as a waitress in a restaurant near a major rapid-transit line; another member frequently stopped in to see her and would then learn and pass on news about the others.

All members sustained the positive personal and social gains they had made in the group. They continued to seek out new pleasant experiences, including family outings and vacations. During stressful periods many were able to ask for therapeutic intervention before reverting back to old behaviors. Appropriate reaching out had replaced destructive striking out.

Conclusion

By the time the meetings were over, the women were no longer using the group primarily as an emotional crutch. By encouraging the social and creative development of the group members, the termination phase was used as a time of transition instead of only as a time of ending. It was the important phase between being in treatment and being an independent, functioning, contributing adult. Though these women originally needed the greater intensity of the insight-oriented discussion group, they made other important gains from the recreational and social aspects of this kind of termination phase. Workers need not think only in terms of "Which kind of group should I offer?" but should also consider "From which kind of group experience can the members benefit most at this time?" As the group-assessment process leads to updated goals, plans for intervention must also remain flexible. Termination need not be viewed primarily as loss, but may also be seen as preparation for a new beginning. The fact that members did not drop out of the group during the last few meetings, as frequently happens in group termination, attests to the positive contribution to individual members that this approach did make. The results were gratifying for everyone involved.

Chapter 8
Individual Assessment and Group-Work Models

Group work may help clients in different ways than casework, but in both methods the clients' ego strength must determine the course and direction of the treatment process. Workers must first assess each client's deficits, conflicts, needs, and abilities in order to offer the most effective intervention.

Parallels do exist between group-work models and casework approaches. A client's capacity for and ability to use relationships to reach treatment goals is similar in both methods. The remedial model incorporates many of the casework practices used with character-disordered clients whose basic anxiety is fear of desertion. Such individuals are capable of making strides with an insight and feeling-oriented approach, although this may only happen after long and painstaking work. The task-oriented group incorporates casework practice principles used with borderline clients who tend to do better with a concrete treatment approach. Their disturbed functioning results from a permeable ego which lives in fear of disintegration or annihilation. The task-oriented group designed to enhance self-image and strengthen coping mechanisms, parallels the more supportive casework treatment to which they can respond.

The remedial discussion group focuses on the intrapsychic dynamics of each member and provides a supportive surrogate-family milieu in which the issues of the past and present can be resolved. In the process, the emotionally deprived parent can give up the repetitive search for the nonexistent, all-giving parent he never had. In Chapter 5, the group treatment phases were linked to stages of grieving for missed childhoods and abandoned hopes. In an accepting atmosphere, the members help each other see through their projection and denial to the feelings of anger, sadness and depression connected with their past experiences. Identifying the source of their feelings frees them to find less damaging ways of expressing them.

This treatment process directly addresses the need of the character disordered person to give up distorting the present in terms of the past. "People in their present life are not perceived or responded to as they actually are but are used as stand-ins for the reenactment of childhood conflicts and defenses."[1] Merl Jackel, in his article,

"Clients with Character Disorders", goes on to point out that this is often mistaken for transference and manipulation. He believes instead that the patterns are acted out unconsciously and indiscriminately in an attempt to reduce frustration or to get needs met. Individuals with character disorders also use massive projection and insist that others must change. The professional therapeutic relationship can serve as a model of interpersonal give and take, thereby interrupting the client's old destructive relationship patterns. Character disordered parents, who have the potential for growth through introspection, appear to make strides more quickly in a remedial group setting than in one-to-one treatment. The nonnurturing mothers were often able to accept challenges to their defenses by their peers long before they could from a social worker. The group facilitated the members' ability to respond affectively and, through the grieving process, correct distorted perceptions and modify maladaptive patterns of behavior.

Over a five-year period the dropouts from the discussion group were the borderline mothers who were unable to meet the group's demands to talk about past and present experiences, behaviors, and feelings. Unable to develop self-awareness in individual sessions, they were equally unable to do so in an introspective discussion group. The borderline client may confuse reality and fantasy and omit or deny factual information. He may exhibit inappropriate, maladaptive, rigid behavior which can be a part of his defensive structure to ward off threatening underlying feelings or hide a fragmented, poor self-image.

Such borderline clients were better served in the task-oriented group where individual problems and feelings are not elicited. The worker must keep the group focused on the task and resist the temptation to permit the members to focus on personal problems, even when this begins to happen naturally as they become more comfortable with one another. Parents who are ready to look inward can be referred to a discussion group.

The task-oriented group designed to enhance ego strength through concrete achievements parallels individual treatment designed to help the client cope with concrete realities. The borderline mothers who have successfully used this group-work model need restitutive work to strengthen their egos before they can modify their defenses to make more appropriate judgments, and take more appropriate actions. They have difficulty sustaining relationships on a normal give-

and-take basis and relate more easily around the situational problems and material in the task group. Anger is the predominant affect with borderline clients and within a structured situation they are helped to control their aggression.

All of the mothers in the task-oriented group expressed enthusiasm about participating but dropped out if the contract was renegotiated with an introspective focus. They were not ready for a remedial group which requires the ability to risk exposure and tolerate intimacy.

CASE ILLUSTRATIONS

Smith Case – Remedial Group

Mrs. Smith had an alcoholic father and a rejecting mother. She was the only daughter and the oldest of four children. From an early age she was burdened with responsibility beyond her years and was often left alone with her brothers at night while her mother worked as a cocktail waitress. Her mother continually found fault with what she did not do and degraded her for what she did do. Her mother wanted her to be like the little girl next door, a "prima ballerina". Instead, Mrs. Smith was a gangling tomboy who preferred to play baseball and to climb trees. Her father was in and out of the home. When he was there, he showered her with attention, and often took her to baseball games or into a local bar. Mrs. Smith worshipped this absent father figure with whom she shared more of a friendship than a father-daughter relationship, and she blamed her mother for her feelings of desertion.

In an attempt to receive the love she never got at home, she married, at age 16, an alcoholic man who was abusive of her. Billy, the second child of that marriage, was conceived in what Mrs. Smith describes as a rape by her husband right after their separation. Billy is perceived as being just like his father, a troublemaker, someone that you cannot count on, and he is scapegoated in the family system. He accepts his role in the family and acts it out by running away, stealing, and keeping the family in a general state of chaos.

Shortly after her divorce became final, Mrs. Smith married a man ten years her senior. Mr. Smith, an insecure man, had never been married before and had a pattern of drifting from job to job. He was the youngest in a large rural family. His father had worked hard as a carpenter, held positions of community leadership, drank heavily, and gave no time to his family. Mr. Smith's mother had set him up continually to win approval by pleasing his father from whom he received no recognition. When Mr. Smith was 13, his mother died of cancer after a long illness, and he lived with a maternal aunt throughout his adolescence. During the first few years of his marriage, Mr. Smith held a steady job in a factory and he and his wife bought a home. They had two children and Mrs. Smith was pregnant at the time of agency intervention.

The family was referred for service when Billy's stepfather beat him with a belt for truancy. Billy was 11 at the time. This episode of loss of control came shortly after Mr. Smith's maternal aunt died, and at a time when he was out of work because of a back injury. He had been hospitalized and was recovering at home. His limited compensation added financial pressure to a pattern of overspending and the family was in danger of losing their home.

In the Smith family the parents do not distort the child's behavior, but rather displace their anger associated with prior objects and situations onto the child. The goal of treatment is to help the clients gradually gain self-awareness about the source of their anger so that they can find less destructive ways of expressing it.

The basic anxiety of parents with character disorders is the fear of abandonment. Many of them have experienced the death or desertion of a parent at an early age, and they talk a great deal about their early deprivations. Unlike borderline clients, they do not need to deny the facts; however, they are not in touch with their true feelings about their past. As Beatrice Reiner and Irving Kaufman state:

> The trauma often includes the actual or emotional loss of parents. In our cases, the adult clients reacted as if they had been abandoned by their parents – even though the latter might be dead – and were searching for them. They seemed angry at the loss and did not, as a general rule, show the usual affective reaction. Instead, they denied the feeling of loss while attempting to deal with it in various substitutive ways.[2]

With both Mr. and Mrs. Smith the emotional loss was experienced as the lack of a consistent caring parental figure with whom to identify. For Mr. Smith this trauma was compounded by the illness and death of his mother in his early teens.

When feelings about the painful past and the missed childhood have not been worked through, denial, projection, and displacement are utilized excessively, often resulting in chaotic, destructive patterns of interactions. Initially, this couple felt completely justified in their anger and behavior toward Billy. He was "asking for it" by his bad behavior. They projected blame for all the problems in their lives onto others, and their solution was for others to change. Mrs. Smith had a running battle going with a family up the street, because they would take Billy in after a family argument. Mrs. Smith felt that their troubles would be over if "those people" would mind their own business. Initially the worker must be careful not inadvertently to strengthen maladaptive defenses in the name of environmental manipulation. The mother's position must be recognized as a defense against her own underlying anxiety, even though there may be some truth to the complaints about "the others". The massive projection can be penetrated very gradually as a solid, trusting casework relationship develops.

Forming an effective therapeutic relationship is often a long and complicated process. The client wishes the relationship to be nurturing but also expects that the worker will be rejecting or depriving just like the original parent. As Beatrice Reiner and Irving Kaufman state:

> The client immediately begins to struggle with the conflict between her wish for gratification and her expectation of rejection. Contact with the worker is perceived as dangerous as well as desirable.

It is not uncommon for the parent to engineer his own rejection, resulting in the continual feeling of deprivation; hence the repetition unless someone breaks the cycle. It is the aim of therapy to help the parent correct the distortion in the treatment relationship. Self-awareness begins to develop on the experiential level. Flexibility and patience are important in establishing a successful treatment relationship. Beatrice Reiner and Irving Kaufman state that the worker must be "warm without being seductive, firm without being punitive, and accepting of the client's feelings without having to identify with his modes of behavior".[4]

70

The worker did not condone physical punishment but the feelings behind the behavior were acknowledged as valid in the face of Billy's acting-out. Mrs. Smith could join the worker in talking about how strained the family relationship had become. It took many hours of casework, spanning almost a year, however, before Mrs. Smith could trust her social worker and really commit herself to the treatment process.

Mrs. Smith had difficulty in moving to the affective level in the casework relationship. She continued to struggle with her strong fears of rejection by her very feminine female worker. She was threatened by the worker's soft, caring manner, and simultaneously aspired to be more like her. If the worker understands what is going on and if the client's feelings have not been repressed, the worker can begin to deal with the underlying affects.

Beatrice Reiner and Irving Kaufman state:

> "In dealing with clients with character disorders, one endeavors to convey that he understands the emotion, which is usually conscious or partially conscious. Because the client's ego is so weak, he cannot deal with the emotion by himself. The worker, by empathizing with the fear, can give the client the support he needs to experience the emotion rather than to run away from it."[5]

It was during the process of using the relationship to get behind the defense to the motivating affects that the caseworker referred Mrs. Smith to the remedial group.

In the remedial group Mrs. Smith experienced an atmosphere of acceptance and mutual support, and the empathy of others who have had similar losses and feelings. Through the total group process as well as the individual relationships within the group, Mrs. Smith was encouraged to feel emotions rather than run away from them. The atmosphere created by the milieu allowed her to make more intensive use of the casework relationship and move to the affective level of treatment.

This movement was facilitated by Mrs. Smith's interaction with another group member who was angry, domineering and aggressive, and with whom she competed for the role of natural leader. Their argumentative bantering entertained the group but also held up the group process. The caseworker began hearing about this group member in individual sessions. With knowledge of the group process obtained from the group worker, the caseworker began to explore with Mrs. Smith her feelings about this member and why she had such an angry response to her. After two or three casework interviews, Mrs. Smith began to realize that this other member reminded her of her mother. This awareness allowed her to be much more direct with the member about her feelings toward her. The hostile, competitive, challenging interaction changed into constructive confrontation and consequently helped the other member to express her own anger verbally rather than act it out behaviorally.

With her caseworker Mrs. Smith continued to talk about her relationship with her mother and began to express anger, resentment and disappointment about that relationship. On an affective level the casework treatment process directly parallels the grieving process linked to the remedial group model. The client must not only grieve for missed experiences, but also for the giving-up of the wish for the nonexistent loving parent. As Mrs. Smith accepted the realities of her maternal relationship, she began to confront her most difficult task in treatment, giving up the wish for her idealized father.

Mrs. Smith began to make exaggerated demands for attention on the male group worker, in keeping with the patterns in her idealized relationship with her father. Attempting to get a sympathetic response from the male group worker, she distorted the female caseworker's reaction to a situation, interpreting the reaction as showing a lack of concern. Once her repetitive patterns were identified by the two workers, they were able to help Mrs. Smith confront the realities about her father and give up the wish that he would rescue her as she perceived he had done so many times. If the emotional losses are successfully mourned, the parent is able to move on to life's new opportunities and challenges. The parent will no longer have to repeat the old patterns in an attempt to make up for what she didn't get the first time.

In the final phase of group treatment, the mutual empathy and support that takes place in the intimacy stage of group development enables the members to pull each other out of depression and sadness and into a period of consolidating constructive coping mechanisms and transferring interactional skills learned in the group to their own personal relationships. The final phase of casework with the Smith family paralleled and supported the group experience. The caseworker began to hold joint sessions with the parents to focus on their communication skills with each other and with their children. During Mrs. Smith's group experience, Billy was seen at a local community agency. Toward the end of treatment, family meetings were held, in which Billy's counselor was included. This was primarily to help Billy and his parents integrate their treatment experiences into their family system, to assume new roles and strengthen interactional skills.

Jones Case – Task-Oriented Group

The Jones family was referred to Children's Protective Services because Stephen, age 6, sustained serious burns of glovelike appearance on both of his hands. Stephen is the third child and the only boy. His sisters resemble their father, who is a large robust man, while Stephen resembles his mother, who is tiny and frail. Stephen was conceived during a period of marital discord and born during a period of parental separation. The marital discord was precipitated by the father's losing his job; consequently, many of the items the family was buying on time were repossessed. This was very upsetting to Mrs. Jones, to whom material possessions are extremely important. She is a compulsive, immaculate housekeeper. One could literally eat off her kitchen floor. Her excessive need for order and cleanliness reflects her attempt to gain control over her own internal anxieties.

When child abuse is a manifested symptom, the parent's perceptions of the child are a good dignostic clue to the level of ego functioning. This mother sees Stephen as a bad, sneaky, manipulative child who lies. She feels that he does things intentionally to hurt her. She gets inordinately upset over an untied shoelace, a ripped school bag or a missing button. She often perceives the ordinary mishaps of a first or second grader as personal attacks. The worker's perception of Stephen is quite different. He is withdrawn but delights in any attention paid to him. He has a strong desire to please and when addressed directly responds straightforwardly. He has not shown manipulative behavior with the worker or in school. He is a child who tries very hard to please his mother. He is confused because nothing he does seems to be right. As a result he gets very depressed and spends long periods of time alone in his room.

Stephen's withdrawn behavior increases his mother's anxiety and brings out her anger. Mrs. Jones has unconsciously chosen to project onto Stephen the "bad" side of herself. Stephen's depression mirrors her internal feelings, which threaten to overwhelm, and which she needs to externalize.

As a very young child Mrs. Jones did not experience the world as a safe place. The youngest of eight children, she had inconsistent early mothering which lacked warmth. Her father died when she was 3 years old after a long illness. Following his death her mother suffered a severe depression and Mrs. Jones was reared by a string of siblings. During her father's illness she was punished for age-appropriate behavior because of the need for quiet in the household. Consequently, she felt herself to be the cause of their father's death. This early trauma left her with intense feelings of anxiety. In order to deal with those feelings she externalizes and attacks them as she projects them onto her son. The fragility of her ego is particularly evident at times of great stress. At those times she perceives Stephen as a monster capable of hurting or killing her.

Irving Kaufman states:

> A group of parents who abuse their children reveal a disturbance in their reality testing. They show a reversal in parent-child roles and perceive their child as big and powerful and themselves as weak and helpless. At times of stress, they develop an episodic psychosis and attack their child out of the delusion that they are protecting themselves from being destroyed.[6]

For Mrs. Jones the internal stress was intensified when her husband, a quiet, passive man who liked to be "out with the boys," emotionally or physically deserted her. Stephen is physically at risk when his mother's intrapsychic problems are exacerbated by interactional tension.

The goal of improving the mother-son relationship cannot be reached by confronting the distortions, because they are the coping mechanisms used to ward off depression. As Irving Kaufman states: "Awareness of the reality aspects of the pathologic features in their relationship to their parents would probably precipitate a severe depression."[7] Our therapeutic objective is, as Robert Knight writes in his article "Borderline States," to strengthen the client's ego so that he can control his behavior. This is done by educating the client in the use of new controls and adaptive methods of relating. Therapists should not attack maladaptive defenses without introducing better substitutes for them.[8] The worker must respect the defenses and improve the pervasive relationship difficulties by focusing on present realities; establishing cause-and-effect understanding so the parent can gradually see that others are not intentionally trying to cause him harm. The worker does not try to get behind defenses and expose the pain of the past but rather tries to build a relationship which will serve as a corrective experience. Then the parent may begin to chart alternative ways of behaving to get the desired result from the child, neighbor, school official, and so on.

The relationship between the worker and the parent is extremely important, since much of the treatment takes place in interpersonal transactions. The quality of the relationship should be one of consistent, concerned caring. The worker should also present himself as a real person with strengths and weaknesses, however. This is important because the client may project omnipotent fantasies onto the worker. The concrete availability of the worker may bring up in the parent awareness and feelings of early deprivation, and the worker may receive excessive demands and become the object of overt hostility.

Irving Kaufman states:

> The hostility in the instance serves as a defense against the underlying depression. In treatment, it is most important that the therapist not respond with counter-hostility or try to bring out further aggression; he must realize that the aggression is a defense mechanism designed to keep the ego intact.

When the goal is to establish trust, the question of how long to sustain the dependent relationship and when to begin to set limits is a difficult one. If reality parameters have been established in the beginning, the answer should flow naturally as the primary treatment relationship is used to look at the other maladaptive relationships in the mother's life. The worker becomes a role model both within the treatment relationship, by not reacting in a hostile or punitive way to provocative behavior, and also through specific discussions on how the mother can avoid hostile confrontations which lead to alienation and isolation. The worker must get to know the details of the mothers's daily life; by knowing what goes wrong and when, the worker helps develop better ways of interaction. It is with the parent that the worker organizes events into a cause-and-effect pattern. If the parent can begin to see how trouble occurs, then she may be able to take an alternate course of action. The mother gradually begins to emulate the worker in her dealings with her child and her community. It is through the processes of identification and incorporation in a relationship that a child is protected and not by introducing threats of punishment to the parent, which only increase her life-threatening anxiety.

Protective social workers are not miracle workers and may not always be able to assess serious danger accurately. Stephen's hands were burned again. The parents were very upset and voluntarily placed their child in a residential setting. This tragedy precipitated a commitment from both of these parents to work on their own relationship. The parents were seen individually and as a couple over a two-year period. Mrs. Jones became able to directly express her needs and expectations to her husband. He changed jobs to get more security and took a more active role in the family as husband and father. As the marital relationship stabilized, the focus turned toward reuniting and strengthening their family. A coordinated effort was made by the residential center and the agency to increase the opportunities for Stephen and his parents to interact. The parents were helped to plan specific family outings.

As part of the work toward reintegration of Stephen into his home, the caseworker referred Mrs. Jones to a task-oriented group to plan a children's Christmas party at the agency. This group was introduced to complement the structured, concrete approach of the casework. As discussed in Chapter 4, the task-oriented group is nonthreatening for clients who have major relationship problems, because it provides an experience in which they can interact around issues other than their problems. This mother still needed her rigid defense system to ward off anxiety and fear and would not have been able to sustain membership in a group dealing with affective material.

Mrs. Jones rediscovered her artistic talent in this group. She took responsibility for making all the invitations and involved her family in the task in between meetings. The invitations were beautiful and she received recognition from the staff, the group, and from many of the 150 families invited. Mrs. Jones was also able to try out other social skills at the party itself. The mothers who planned the party decided to rent costumes for the entertainment. She was dressed as

Bugs Bunny and had big ears and a fluffy tail. Hidden from view, she was able to risk interacting freely with the children. She delighted in the demands of the children and having her tail pulled, interactions which a few years previous would have caused rage. The task-group experience gave this mother a tremendous feeling of achievement and confidence during an anxiety-ridden period of self-doubt about her child's return home. It helped make Stephen's reintegration a success.

Chapter 9
Summary And Conclusions

Nonnurturing parents can be helped to change and grow through group experiences. Frequently incapable of overcominng the emotional deficits of their beginning years, they reach adulthood unable to attain satisfying relationships with friends and family members. Trapped in their social and emotional isolation, they remain destructive to themselves and their children. Group experiences offer opportunities for relief from the burdens of their special kind of loneliness.

For decades abusive and neglectful parents were perceived as unreachable by mental-health professionals who frequently extended too limited a range of interventive approaches. Experience has shown that this population can be helped, though not necessarily through the traditional treatment modalities offered to verbal middle-class clients who seek help for a presenting problem.

The nonnurturing parents who can look inward and express themselves verbally can be served through the remedial problem-focused group. Other parents who are less verbal, or who cannot identify their personal problems, can be helped through other kinds of group experiences.

Many previously "unreachable" clients have demonstrated a responsiveness to the developmental or socialization group-work model which uses activities as a therapeutic tool. The activities enhance the social aspect of the group, permit interpersonal distance, and heighten a sense of mastery. Activities can also increase self-awareness as members are helped to understand the meaning of their behavior patterns.

The social-goals or task-oriented group is still further removed from an affective or insight orientation. In this group a specific goal is to be reached through a division of labor. Activities are not used to enhance self-awareness but instead to convert "self-seeking into social contribution."[1] Therapy is linked to successful task completion.

Each of these groups may be the major treatment for a client or a steppingstone to something else. For example, the task-oriented group has facilitated both movement into an intensive group experience for some members and encouraged the transfer from therapeutic to community supports for others. If the group as a whole is ready for a change, the worker may initiate a renegotiation of the working agreement and, together with the members, redirect the focus of the group interactions.

It has been observed that character-disordered clients respond more quickly to the inwardly focused remedial discussion group than to the equivalent approach in casework treatment. The more disturbed borderline personality can do better in the task-oriented group where painful, threatening feelings are not elicited.

Many social workers in recent years have developed new and creative group services for this difficult-to-serve population.

The California Foothill Family Service in Pasadena designed a family-care program "to ameliorate the problem of child battering."[2] It offered a series of daytime weekend experiences, with planned activites for parents and children. Traditional casework, group work and family-life education were blended with nontraditional uses of recreation, music and art, and utilitarian classes in budgeting and nutrition. Differential group experiences were a major part of this 120-hour program. Within professionally led discussion groups, parents could express frustrations about their children, their marriage, or about parenting in general. An educationally focused group taught specific parenting skills. A third group used didactic and experimental techniques to emphasize (1) self-esteem, (2) self-gratification, (3) mutual sharing, and (4) empowerment.

The Child Sexual Abuse Treatment Program at the Santa Clara County Juvenile Probation Department in San Jose, California, provides group counseling to the sexually abused child and his family. The program views incestuous behavior as one of many symptoms of family dysfunction. Therapy replaces legal punishment and family separation as a deterrent to sexual abuse. The therapeutic program is based of the theory and methods of humanistic psychology which promotes growth and self-management. Family members are seen individually, as couples, as families or as groups of families, depending upon the special needs of each case.

Parents United and Daughters United are self-help organizations which grew out of this program. Their development was prompted by the need for sympathetic and supportive others to help the victims and witnesses of abuse through critical periods. Older members help newcomers to develop a positive consciousness about themselves and the direction of their lives.[3]

Parents Anonymous, the most well known of self help groups, has become a major source of support for this population. The first Parents Anonymous Chapter was started in the early 1970's by a woman named Jolly K., who was frustrated and angry that there were no resources specifically designed to help abusive parents stop hurting their children. She decided to start her own group with the help of her psychiatric social worker, Leonard Lieber. The group was to be a place to discuss the feelings associated with being an abusive parent.

In 1974 Parents Anonymous received its first grant from the federal government and today there are over 800 chapters helping over 8,000 parents deal with their problems. Each group has a parent chairperson who leads the group. Each group is also sponsored by a professional who acts as a consultant in support of the parent chairperson. The sponsor is usually a social service provider who can refer parents to additional resources beyond the P.A. experience.

Many P.A. groups have expanded their activities beyond the once a week meeting to support services. Such services included: parent education classes, emergency services funds, Parent Advocates to respond to crises and help parents deal with agencies and liaison programs with related resources such as Alcoholics Anonymous and Head Start. Parents Anonymous also hopes to form chapters in prisons for parents who have been incarcerated for child abuse.[4]

In Massachusetts, an innovative social worker with the Department of Public Welfare provides a family model which incorporates a mothers-daughters discussion group and a fathers discussion group in the treatment of incestuous families. She has also designed and organized a group for parents who have been separated from their children. This educationally focused model instructs parents in what they have to do to "get their kids back," and attempts to help them develop a positive rather than adversary relationship with the Department of Public Welfare. Each group of parents meets for eight sessions, with an assigned topic for each meeting.[5]

These are but a few examples of social-service settings which are recognizing and accepting their mandated responsibility to deal with child abuse and which are creatively using group services to that end. The laws which protect the rights of children confer upon any social agency, and the worker who represents that agency, the right to stay with the situation until at least the minimum of care and protection of the child is assured.

Annie Lee Sandusky asserts that:

> The knowledge, skills, and creativity of the worker, his clearness and conviction about his responsibilities under the law or charter, and the support of the agency through its structure, policies and procedures are the factors that assure effective results.[6]

Communities must commit a wide range of coordinated social services if they want to prevent or ameliorate child abuse and neglect. In conjunction with the delivery of other important services such as individual counseling, foster care, medical services, homemaker services, day care, parent education and job counseling and training, groups can be used in many innovative ways. Local community health centers, which are replacing the neighborhood houses as community focal points, could set up store-front drop-in centers where mothers and children could be helped to develop constructive relationships with their neighbors. Prenatal clinics should establish supportive groups (either discussion or activity) for high-risk mothers. Preschools and public schools could do the same.

Mental health professionals must continue to create and deliver interventive approaches that can be understood and accepted by the families to be served. Ultimately it is the strength of these families, their willingness to work and their desire to grow that gives social workers the inspiration to structure the opportunities in which growth can occur.

NOTES

Chapter 1

1. Lloyd De Mause, "The Nightmare of Childhood," in *The Children's Rights Movement*, ed. by Beatrice Gross and Ronald Gross, Anchor Press/Doubleday, New York: 1977, p. 29.

2. *Ibid.* p. 30.

3. Robert H. Bremner, ed., *Children and Youth in America: A Documentary History*, Vol. I, Harvard University Press, Cambridge, Mass.: 1974, p. 38.

4. Massachusetts Society for the Prevention of Cruelty to Children, "Children: Our Past, Our Promise," Boston, 1978, p. 2.

5. Bremner, *Children and Youth in America*, Vol. II, p. 186.

6. MSPCC, *op. cit.* p. 3.

7. Bremner, *op. cit.* p. 192.

8. Helen Harris Perlman, "Social Casework," in *Encyclopedia of Social Work*, Vol. XIV, National Association of Social Workers, New York: 1968, p. 710.

9. *Ibid.* p. 710.

10. Annie Lee Sandusky, "Protective Services," in *Encyclopedia of Social Work*, Vol. XIV, National Association of Social Workers, New York: 1968, p. 579.

11. Perlman, *op. cit.* p. 711-712.

12. Bremner, *Children and Youth in America*, Vol. III, p. 853.

13. Perlman, *op. cit.*, p. 713.

14. U.S. Department of Health, Education and Welfare, Pub. #75-30073, "Child Abuse and Neglect: The Problem and Its Management," Vol. I, Washington, D.C.: 1976, p. 32.

15. *Ibid.* p. 4.

16. Robert Mulford, "Protective Services for Children," in *Encyclopedia of Social Work*, National Association of Social Workers, Washington, D.C.: 1974, p. 1009.

17. Sandusky, *op. cit.* p. 580.

18. Robert M. Friedman, "Child Abuse: A Review of the Psychosocial Research," Institute for Behavioral Research, Inc., Silver Spring, Maryland: 1975, p. 4-5.

19. U.S. Dept. HEW, *op. cit.* p. 3.

20. Norman Polansky, "Help for the Helpless," Paper presented at Centennial Symposium, Massachusetts Society for the Prevention of Cruelty to Children, Boston, Mass., October, 1978, p. 3.

Chapter 2

1. Robert M. Friedman, "Child Abuse: A Review of the Psychosocial Research," Institute for Behavioral Research, Inc., Silver Spring, Maryland, 1975, p. 59-60.

2. David Gil, *Violence Against Children*, Harvard University Press, Cambridge, Mass., 1970, p.12.

3. Friedman, *op. cit.* pp. 60-61.

4. Dana Ackley, "A Brief Overview of Child Abuse," *Social Casework*, Vol. 58, No. 1, January 1977, p. 21.

5. D. Bakan, *Slaughter of the Innocents*, Jossey-Bass, San Francisco, 1971, p. 116.

6. M.G. Morris and R.W. Gould, "Role Reversal: A Necessary Concept in Dealing with the Battered Child Syndrome'," in *The Neglected/Battered Child Syndrome*, Child Welfare League of America, New York, 1963, p. 28.

7. B.F. Steele and C.B. Pollock, "A Psychiatric Study of Parents who Abuse Infants and Small Children," in R.E. Helfer and C.H. Kempe (eds), *The Battered Child*, University of Chicago Press, Chicago, 1968, pp. 109-110.

8. Ackley, *op. cit.*, p. 22.

9. *Ibid.* p. 22.

10. Norman Polansky, "Help for the Helpless," Paper Presented at Centennial Symposium, Massachusetts Society for the Prevention of Cruelty to Children, Boston, Mass., October, 1978, p. 11.

11. Friedman, *op. cit.* p. 61.

12. Gil, *op. cit.* p. 12.

13. Gil, *op. cit.* p. 10.

14. Gil, *op. cit.* p. 13.

Chapter 3

1. Irvin D. Yalom, *The Theory and Practice of Group Psychotherapy,* Basic Books Inc. New York: 1970, p. 39

2. Gisela, Konopka, *Social Group Work: A Helping Process*, Prentice-Hall, Inc., Englewood Cliffs, N.J.; 1972, p. 30.

3. Erik H. Erikson, *Childhood and Society*, W.W. Norton & Co., Inc., New York: 1963, p. 266-67.

4. *Ibid*, p. 267.

5. Yalom, *op. cit.* p. 5.

6. Arthur Blum, "The Aha' Response as a Therapeutic Goal," in *Group Work as Part of Residential Treatment*, ed. Henry W. Maier, NASW, New York: 1965, p. 47.

7. James A. Garland, Hubert E. Jones & Ralph L. Kolodny, "A Model for Stages of Development in Social Work Groups," in *Explorations in Group Work*, ed. Saul Bernstein; Charles River Books, Inc., Boston: 1976, pp. 50-51.

8. Joann Cook and Sharrell Munce, "Group Treatment For Abusive Parents: Creating a New Family System," in *Family Health Care: Health Promotion and Illness Care*, ed. Robert Jackson & Jean Morton, Univ. of California, Berkeley: 1976, p. 137.

9. Yalom, *op. cit.* p. 21.

10. *Ibid*, P. 22.

11. *Ibid*, P. 56.

12. *Ibid*, P. 72.

13. Robert Paradise & Robert Daniels, "Group Composition as a Treatment Tool With Children," in *Further Explorations in Group Work*, ed. by Saul Bernstein, Charles River Books, Inc., Boston: 1976, p. 41.

Chapter 4

1. Catherine Pappell & Beulah Rothman, "Social Group Work Models: Possession and Heritage," *Journal of Education for Social Work*, Vol. II, #2, Fall, 1966.

2. James Garland; Hubert Jones and Ralph Kolodny, "A Model for Stages of Group Development," in *Explorations in Group Work*, Saul Bernstein, ed., Charles River Books, Inc., Boston: 1976.

6. Irving Kaufman, "The Physically Abused Child," in *Child Abuse: Intervention and Treatment*, ed. by Nancy B. Ebeling and Deborah A. Hill, Publishing Sciences Group, Inc., Acton, Mass.: 1975, p. 86.

7. Irving Kaufman, "Therapeutic Considerations of the Borderline Personality Structure," in *Ego Psychology and Dynamic Casework*, ed. by Howard J. Parad, Family Service Association of America, New York; 1958, p. 104.

8. Robert Knight, "Borderline States," *Bulletin of the Menninger Clinic*, Vol. 17, No. 1, January 1953, p. 11.

9. Kaufman, *op. cit.* p. 108.

Chapter 9

1. Catherine Pappell and Beulah Rothman, "Social Group Work Models: Possession and Heritage," Journal of Education for Social Work, Vol. II, No. 2, Fall, 1966, p. 68.

2. Audrey Oppenheimer, "Triumph Over Trauma in the Treatment of Child Abuse," Social Casework, Vol. 59, No. 6, June, 1978, pp. 353-355.

3. Henry Giarretto, "The Treatment of Father Daughter Incest: A Psychosocial Approach," *Children Today*, Vol. V, No. 4, July-August, 1976, pp. 3-4.

4. Kee MacFarlane and Leonard Lieber, "Parents Anonymous: The Growth of An Idea," U.S. Department of Health, Education and Welfare, National Center of Child Abuse, Publication Number (OHDS) 78-30086, June, 1978, pp. 3-4.

5. Mary Devlin and Michael Gray, "What'll I Have To Do To Get My Kids Back?: The Answer", unpublished paper, Department of Public Welfare, Protective Service Unit, Brockton, Mass., 1979, pp. 2-12.

6. Annie Lee Sandusky, "Protective Services," in *Encyclopedia of Social Work*, Vol. 15, National Association of Social Workers, New York, 1968, p. 580.